Reaching for Comfort
What I Saw, What I Learned, and How I Blew it Training as a Pastoral Counselor

Sherri Mandell

Teaneck, New Jersey

REACHING FOR COMFORT ©2021 Sherri Mandell. All rights reserved. No part of this book may be used or reproduced in any manner whatsoever without written permission except in the case of brief quotations embodied in critical articles and reviews.

Published by Ben Yehuda Press
122 Ayers Court #1B
Teaneck, NJ 07666

http://www.BenYehudaPress.com

To subscribe to our monthly book club and support independent Jewish publishing, visit patreon.com/BenYehudaPress

Ben Yehuda Press books may be purchased at a discount by synagogues, book clubs, and other institutions buying in bulk. For information, please email markets@BenYehudaPress.com

ISBN13: 978-1-934730-81-2

21 22 23 / 10 9 8 7 6 5 4 3 2 1   20210218

Contents

Part I

1. First Words	1
2. Dismissed	7
3. The Underworld	14
4. Class	19
5: A Voice of Comfort	30
6. Cooking Without Fire	37
7. A Mistake	42
8. Looking the Wrong Way	50
9. Drinking Coffee with a Patient	55
10. Naked	61
11. Imagining Death	66
12. Pastoral Care	72
13. Strawberries	76
14. The Beauty that is Swallowed in the Darkness	84

Part II

15. Moving His Lips	89
16. The Rock on the Well	98
17. Singing to the Soul	102
18. A Form of Madness	109
19. Kissing Back	113
20. Ordinary Death	116
21. Dual Citizenship	119
22. Becoming a Patient	124
Abour the Author	137

Also by Sherri Mandell

The Blessing of a Broken Heart
The Road to Resilience: From Chaos to Celebration

Dedication

For my children—Daniel, Eliana and Avraham, and Gabi and Pliah—and my grandchildren—Ori, Yehuda, Lavi, and Tzori—who give me such joy. And for my husband, Seth Mandell, my anchor, my love and my comfort.

Thanks to my friends, Shira Chernoble, Elisabeth Kushner, Ruth Mason, Valerie Seidner, and Roochie Sinai. Thank you to my sisters Nancy Lederman and Loren Fogelson. Thanks to my agent, Anna Olswanger, who worked with such dedication to make sure that this book would be brought into the world. Thanks to the New York Jewish Federation Caring Commission for their support. Thanks to my teachers for giving me guidance and support and the many fine nurses and doctors I had the privilege to work with. And finally, thanks to the patients and their families, many of whom opened their hearts and souls to me.

Note:
All patients that I present in this book are fictional composites, drawn broadly from real stories. All names and identities are changed. Any similarity to specific individuals, living or dead, is coincidental.

About suffering they were never wrong,
The old Masters: how well they understood
Its human position: how it takes place
While someone else is eating or opening a
    window or just walking dully along...
—W.H. Auden, *Musée de Beaux Arts*

Everyone who is born holds dual citizenship, in the kingdom of the well and in the kingdom of the sick. Although we all prefer to use only the good passport, sooner or later each of us is obliged, at least for a spell, to identify ourselves as citizens of that other place.
—Susan Sontag, *Illness As Metaphor*

I will rejoice and delight in Your kindness, for You have seen my affliction; You know the troubles of my soul.
—Psalm 31:8

Chapter 1

First Words

Room 7324. I stepped in slowly. My watch read 2:30 and outside the sun was burning, but inside the room was dark, the overhead light flickering as if it couldn't make up its mind to go on. A woman lay in the bed near the door with the hospital quilt bunched at the end of the bed. The head of the bed was propped up at a 45-degree angle, a light pink sheet covered the mound of her belly. She looked pregnant.

I figured it was her teenage daughter who slouched in an arm chair in the corner of the room, glancing up at me and quickly back to her book as I entered. I got the feeling she had spent enough time here to know when she needed to pay attention.

I introduced myself and told the patient that I was training to be a pastoral counselor. I didn't tell her that she was the first patient I was visiting on my own. I didn't tell her that I had no idea what to say, that I was terrified. She told me that her name was Liz. I was surprised because she spoke in a strong Australian accent.

"Look at me," she said. "I've got this tumor, it came back. It's in my belly. That's why I'm so swollen." She held a half-quart plastic take-out cup with a plastic lid, a straw bobbing out of the bright orange juice. A green plastic tube laced through her nose and looped toward her stomach. "Carrot juice," she said, taking a sip. "I can't take in anything solid. The doctors aren't sure I'll ever be able to eat again."

She said it so matter-of-factly that I didn't know how to answer. I felt the shock and horror of not ever being able to eat again. Not being able to have a breakfast of eggs and toast, not being able to eat spaghetti or steak or French fries or fried rice or eggplant salad. She smiled shyly. I could see childhood in her face. I asked her what she did before she got sick.

She told me that she was a potter, that she wished she had one of her cups there to show me, that she loved working with the earth. "You can turn dirt into gold," she said. "Really. I miss it. I miss it so much. I want to return to my wheel. But the doctors don't give me much hope," she whispered, as if not to worry her daughter. "But only God knows, God is the one who decides. Not the doctors."

"You're right, the doctors don't know everything," I said quietly. Her voice was strong, and her cheeks were pink, and she was so pretty that I believed her—she would survive. According to the form that my teacher had given me, Liz was only 49. Of course, the doctors were wrong.

She sighed: "You don't know how much I just want a normal life. I want to feed my kids, read, go to the movies, water plants; just normal things. I don't need a trip to Paris or Hong Kong. I don't need fancy food or clothes. I want regular things, helping my friends who have been so good to me. I want to make dinner, water a garden, squeeze orange juice. Just the usual things—anything instead of being sick."

"Ordinary life becomes precious," I said, thinking about how in the months following our own tragedy, the murder of my 13-year-old son, mundane routines like laundry and cooking, feeding my family, became anchors to this world.

"Yes, that's it. The doctor told me that even if I get better, I'll never be the same. They're going to have to take something out. My intestines. But I don't believe it. The doctor says I'll have to be hooked up to a colostomy bag. He says that I may not be able to eat solid food. But it's God who decides, not the doctors," she repeated. She put her cup of juice on the tray that looped over the bed, leaned back on the pillow, and smiled at me.

I was horrified at the idea that she would have a colostomy bag, the indignity of walking around with her waste in a bag.

"We're going to be fine. Right, Ami?" she said. Then she turned to me: "She's here every day after school."

Ami looked at her mother and tilted her head to one side and then rolled it slowly forward and then to the other side, and back, making a circle, as if she were working out the tension in her neck.

"I got sick for the first time in Melbourne," Liz said. "I had pains in my belly. I thought it was nothing. But after a while I went to the doctor. I was wrong. I've spent a lot of time in hospitals. The hospital in Melbourne wasn't so great either," she added. "That doctor thought he was it and a bit…remember, Ami?"

Her daughter folded her arms and said: "The doctor there was a jerk." They laughed together.

"My life has been a mess," Liz said. "My husband left me, married Ami's first grade teacher. I still don't believe it. We haven't had an easy time. And I've been sick for a long time. But I can get better," she said. "I can."

"You can," I said.

My head started to pound, the beginning of a headache above my right ear. I told her that I had to go, that I would see her next week but that I hoped that she would be discharged before that.

As I walked outside, even the blast of hot air around my face felt pure and cleansing. I got into my car, put the radio on loud and sang to a Whitney Houston song, *The Greatest Love of All* while I drove…*no matter what they take from me, they can't take away my dignity*. This was years before Whitney Houston's death so there was no feeling of discord or dissonance in the lyrics—just a sense of release and celebration.

Passing the Malcha Mall, I realized that I had a free hour before my youngest, my ten-year-old son Gavi, returned from school. I needed a cup of coffee at a café. I needed to be around people who were not dealing with death and illness.

After I parked and entered the mall, I looked at the people going up and down the escalators, how carefree they were, how beautiful it was to be out, free, drinking coffee, meeting friends.

Like many people, I dislike malls—the high-pitched lighting and the over-processed air and the lack of windows. But that day I was happy to be there. My headache went away.

I walked into the clothing store Zara and noticed a purple velvet jacket I liked, but it was way too expensive, almost as much as I spent in a week for groceries. I couldn't let myself buy it. I wanted that jacket, though. I called my friend Rachel. I told her how much the jacket cost. *Do you think I should buy it?* She said, "No, it's way too expensive."

I walked to a café and sipped a coffee. Suddenly I realized that I had a Zara credit folded in my wallet that would cover half of the cost of the jacket. I returned to the store. But the jacket was gone. They only had extra small, too small for me.

Suddenly I needed that jacket, I had to have the jacket. I needed a purple velvet jacket. I talked to the young, tall, thin salesgirl with fire engine red lips and explained what had happened. "I'll check the changing room," she said.

"I found it," she said a few minutes later when she approached me next to the women's sweaters. "The only size medium left in the store. There's a woman in the dressing room trying it on. I told her somebody wanted it if she doesn't take it."

"Great," I said. Then I realized that the woman in the dressing room could buy that jacket, the last medium in the store. "Go back and tell her I don't want it," I said. "Otherwise she'll definitely want it. You know, the competition."

She nodded and laughed as if we were co-conspirators. I waited for five minutes, ten minutes—the woman in the dressing room didn't bring out the jacket. I had to get home to take care of Gavi.

Then I did something I had never done before. I stepped into the dressing room, squatted and peered under the door of each cubicle to see if I could find my jacket. I hoped nobody was watching. Finally, I gave up and told myself that it was only a jacket, and one I couldn't really afford.

I walked out of the dressing room and as I turned to exit the store, the salesgirl touched my shoulder. "I found one in the back," she said, her red lipstick gleaming under the fluorescent lights. I grabbed the jacket, touching the velvet to my face. This is what I wanted: the feeling that life was gentle, yielding, plush. As if a fabric, a jacket could save me. Could save Liz. I bought the jacket.

The next week when I returned to the hospital, I walked up the seven flights of stairs—I'd already learned not to wait for the elevator because it took so long to come—and entered the small room where we had class. After greeting us, our teacher, Ora, told us that she had bad news. The seven of us sat at the rectangular conference table—we five students and our teachers. My stomach tensed as if there were a clenched fist pounding my insides. "Liz died," she said.

Death had somehow snuck into the hospital and annihilated her, erased her. Michael, the co-teacher, added, "Benjamin, the physics professor, died as well. Death comes in waves at the hospital. It's strange, but sometimes nobody dies for a while and then there are a few people all at once."

I wondered if the angel of death was simply too lazy to be

bothered, so he made his rounds in the most convenient way. I'd visited Benjamin with Michael. He seemed to be in a coma, no movement at all. Death may have announced itself in Benjamin's room but in Liz's, as far as I could tell, death hardly gestured. Even though the signs weren't good, she was still beautiful, alive. I didn't discuss anything with her about death, about saying goodbye. I didn't talk to her daughter. I didn't comfort Liz.

In class I was too stunned to concentrate as we talked about Liz and Benjamin and said a prayer for them—that their souls should rise to heaven. And then my classmate, Ruth, began to speak quietly. She told us that she'd visited Liz the day before she died. "Poor thing. She was in a lot of pain and she looked straight at me—very intensely. Liz told me that the night before she had left her body and looked at herself from above, from the ceiling, she could see herself lying in the bed. I wondered whether she meant that she was leaving her body, that she was dying—or was it pain that was causing her to disassociate? I could see that she was suffering. I asked her if she wanted me to sing and she said yes. I sang to her and then we sang together, and she smiled as we sang."

I couldn't imagine singing to Liz. I have a terrible voice. But now I felt awful and sad and useless. Ruth had sung with Liz before she died. She provided a few minutes of comfort. And me? I went shopping.

Chapter 2

Dismissed

It was my fourth week at the hospital. My teacher Michael and I sat at a picnic table outside the hospital in a small garden surrounded by a cascade of pink bougainvillea flowers and white rose bushes. A stripe of cirrus clouds sliced the blue sky.

The weather in Israel leaps from six months of a very hot summer to the cold, rainy season of winter without much of a transition. No startling display of colorful autumn leaves. But it was that unique November weather: a crisp, perfect day.

A young man in ripped jeans and a black t-shirt sat on a wooden bench, smoking. People always smoke outside the hospital. After being close to illness, you would think they would quit immediately. Instead the hospital seemed to have the opposite effect.

"Last week a woman jumped from her window and fell right by here and died," Michael said.

It didn't surprise me. It was easy to imagine that pain could lead a person to want to get out of here in any way she could.

Michael and I walked back into the hospital to the oncology ward, past a man who was playing backgammon with a patient in a bathrobe. The game was spread in front of them; the patient tossed the dice onto the board. The man he was playing with had very short gray hair, a buzz cut, and was wearing a well-worn brown leather jacket with side pockets. His jacket squeaked when he raised his hand to wave. He looked like a worn-out boxer, as if he could do a side step and throw a punch. "Hey Ezra," Michael said. "I haven't seen you here in a while. How are you?" They shook hands. Ezra stood up and Michael embraced him.

Then Ezra's face turned red. "I'm so angry I could eat a wall," he seethed. "I had to wait here for four hours this morning. Since 7:00 am. I can't stand this place." Ezra rubbed his bloodshot eyes.

Michael spoke softly, "That's a long time to wait."

Ezra's voice got louder. "I can't tolerate liars. That woman is a liar. I don't have an authorization for the treatment from my insurance because it's experimental and the hospital didn't want to give it to me.

"This hospital is horrible, and I had to wait all morning, and nobody cares. I didn't get my treatment. Look at this. Make a copy of it and read it." He shoved the paper toward Michael.

Then he glanced my way. "Who are you? Are you a social worker?"

"This is Sherri," Michael explained. "She's training to be a pastoral counselor."

"Oh, I thought she was a social worker." He spoke about me as if I weren't there.

Michael put his hand on Ezra's shoulder. "Ezra, it looks like you're having a hard day. I'm not going to make a copy of this paper. But there's somebody to complain to. Leah is the head of the ward, and she needs to know about this. You really should tell her."

"No way. She lies right out to me."

He folded his arms across his belly, and his mood seemed to shift because he smiled at us. "You know this story? There's a group of religious Jews on a boat, and they eat only kosher food. The rabbi talks to the captain so that he will prepare special kosher food and take care of them the whole trip—he promises the captain a reward. So the captain gives them special service and lets them eat at his own table—steak, lamb, ribs, everything perfectly done. Dessert. The rabbi puts his arms around the captain, tells him he'll take care of him when the time comes.

"At the end of the trip, when the people walk off the ship, the captain is waiting and waiting for his tip and the rabbi nods at him and walks by, instead of tipping. The captain keeps waiting.

'Finally, the rabbi understands, and he comes back and gives him a lot of money—more than the captain was expecting—and the captain says: 'You people may not have killed Christ, but you definitely drove him crazy!!!'"

He laughed and the corners of his eyes wrinkled. He wiped his eyes and looked at me: "You're not laughing. Did you understand?"

"I didn't understand the ending."

"How long have you been in Israel?"

"Nine years," I said.

"Why don't you learn Hebrew?" he asked.

Of course, we were speaking in Hebrew. But he was right. My Hebrew wasn't great. I have a very strong American accent and my verb tenses are often incorrect. How would I ever be able to talk to people here? I spoke English most of the time, even in Israel. I was embarrassed about my lack of fluency in Hebrew, but I didn't say anything. Michael and I walked away.

"He's a good guy," Michael said, "but he can be a real pain in the neck."

Later Michael sent me to the hematology department on the opposite end of the seventh floor from the cancer ward. He told me that I should wander around and see if there was anybody there who wanted to talk. Hematology—diseases of the blood. I knew little about the patients there, but after my encounter with Ezra, I wasn't optimistic about the day.

I walked down a long dark hallway and arrived at a large lounge with leather recliners and a row of plastic chairs. In the middle of the room, a woman who looked to be in her 70s sat with a younger woman.

An IV pole was parked next to the older woman, a bag looped over the metal stand bulging full of burgundy blood. The two women looked alike with wide full faces shaped like apples, caramel brown eyes, and long pale eyelashes.

The mother wore a light blue cashmere bathrobe tied at the waist with a sash, and a layer of moisturizer coated her face, so her skin looked wet. The daughter wore high heels, linen pants, a white fitted shirt with bell sleeves, as if she were dressed for a cruise.

After we greeted each other, I asked about their accent. They told me that they were from Scotland. I explained that I was a pastoral counselor—that I volunteered in the hospital.

The older woman said, "It must be so nice for you to help others, to do charity. You must get a good feeling from it."

I didn't like the word *charity*. I didn't like thinking of myself as a do-gooder, a "goody goody" as my father would have called it—who was here to score brownie points. Or to feed on other people's misery.

I knew it was more complicated. I sensed that there was a reciprocal nature to this work, that there was something I would receive here. I didn't tell them that since my son had been murdered, I could no longer live in the normal world.

The younger woman said, "There was so much traffic today. We came in a taxi and we had to wait behind a truck stuck on the road for twenty minutes. So frustrating."

I didn't want to make small talk, yet I didn't have the courage to probe or question them.

They asked me about my family, I told them I had four children. I didn't tell them that one was dead. They asked whether I was religious. I nodded and they said, "You must find a lot of solace in that."

Again, the answer was more complicated, but I just said yes. I wasn't always religious and becoming a Jew who could pray in Hebrew and invite fifteen people over for a homemade five course Shabbat dinner without anxiety had been a long, complicated process.

They asked where I was from. I told them that we had moved from Silver Spring, Maryland to Israel a few years before. I thought about telling them that that I had taught writing at a university, that I had worked as a humor writer on a website, that my parents had been upset with me for leaving them so far away in Florida. I was relieved when a nurse called them and interrupted our conversation.

I sat down next to a man who looked about thirty. He was tall and thin and had thick curly auburn hair. He told me that his name was Yehuda, and that he was in the hospital to do an experimental treatment for Crohn's disease. I said that I was training to be a spiritual support person.

He said, "Don't bother talking to me. I'm fed up. It's like I'm a broken car. They should just leave me in the dump. I can't eat what I want. I can't eat anything that grows from the ground. Isn't that ridiculous? I should be able to eat what I want. There is no meaning in any of this. None. I'd like to punch God in the face. I'm too young to go through this." He turned to me and the sides of his mouth turned down: "I don't believe in anything."

"You sound really frustrated," I said. I knew I sounded stupid.

"Of course, I am. It's not that I have Crohn's. I *am* Crohn's."

"What do you mean by that?" I said, thinking I had asked a good question.

"You could never understand," he said, scratching his scalp with both hands.

"Maybe not."

"Definitely not. Can you leave me alone?" he asked.

I'd been dismissed. It was so hard to speak. Words were heavy. I was afraid of prying, hurting, saying the wrong thing, saying nothing. Now I understood how people felt around me after Koby's murder, especially in the first years. What can you say to help?

I left the hematology department and returned to the cancer ward and walked into a 95-year-old woman's room. At the sink a woman brushed on makeup in front of a large rectangular mirror. She pursed her lips and smoothed on light pink lipstick and dotted blush from a compact onto her cheeks. She opened her eyes wide to apply a thick coat of mascara.

She was one of the daughters; she must have been in her 60s but she turned to me and began to talk about how healthy her mother had been even with cancer until about a week ago when she had had a stroke. Her mother had cleaned her own house and cooked for the whole family. I couldn't imagine it. She was so old, the woman on the bed, with white hair and a large blue wound mark on her wrinkled forearm.

The woman was hardly moving, hardly breathing. There was the smell of something burning in the room, the gurgle of a small orange bubble-like contraption against the wall. The daughter looked in the mirror and rubbed in the blush. "I don't know how she could get sick so quickly. She was fine. It's just not fair for her to be so sick."

"Can you tell me about your mother?" I asked.

"No," she said, turning to me and then again to the mirror. "I really don't want to. But thanks."

Again I'd been dismissed. I knew that I should feel more sympathetic toward this woman, but her mother was 95. It couldn't come as a surprise that she might die. It just didn't seem that bad to me. The way that my 13-year-old son died was so much worse. The truth was that I didn't have that much compassion for an ordinary death.

Chapter 3

The Underworld

On May 8, 2001, my 13-year-old son Koby cut school and went hiking with his friend Yosef Ish Ran in a canyon near our home in Israel. Terrorists trapped the two eighth-grade boys in a cave and beat them to death with rocks. The murderers smeared the boys' blood on the walls of the cave.

Two young boys who carried their sandwiches, math books, and prayer books inside their backpacks. They were missing all night. It wasn't until daybreak that their bodies were found in a cave in the canyon less than a half a mile from our home.

Nobody is equipped to deal with such horror, but I felt particularly unprepared. I had grown up on Long Island where there had been no tragedies in my life, only the deaths of grandparents in old age. I'd had an all-American childhood. I'd been a cheerleader at Lynbrook High School on Long Island and editor of the high school yearbook. In high school, I'd gone out with a basketball player.

I'd studied at Cornell University, gotten a Master's in Creative Writing, worked as a lecturer in composition and business writing at the University of Maryland. None of that helped me with what I had to face. Nothing prepared me for loss.

And I knew that there were those who blamed me for bringing my children to a dangerous part of the world. But politics was the last thing on my mind. My first birthday without Koby made me happy because I was one year closer to dying.

A rabbi told me that the soul separates from the body at the time of death, so that even though the boys were beaten, they didn't suffer. But I didn't believe it. Much as I wanted to, I knew that Koby had suffered. He'd been tortured. And I hadn't been able to protect him.

There is no place in the soul for the death of a child. He was our oldest, the one who helped me with the other kids, the one who taught me how to be a mother. I had great dreams for him. I thought he would be a lawyer or a judge because he always argued for the children's rights: for a later bedtime, more computer time, more pizza, more Coke.

Once, exasperated with his pleading, I told him that when he was 18, I would buy him a Coke vending machine for his room. Sometimes we would make up stories. I would start with a sentence and then he would add to the story and his additions were always so surprising.

After his murder, we found a folder of jokes on the computer, ones he had gathered and saved, his favorites. Like this:

As the light changed from red to green to yellow and back to red again, I sat there thinking about life. Was it nothing more than a bunch of honking and yelling? Sometimes it just seems that way.

It wasn't really a joke, but it made sense that he would like a statement like that because he was precocious. He'd taped *New Yorker* cartoons all over the walls of his bedroom in Israel, when he was only 13. One of them showed the leaning tower of Pisa—only it was the people who were leaning, not the tower. Of course, he also taped posters of Michael Jordan to his wall.

He was a normal teenager and I yearned for him. In some ways, I wanted to die with him, but I had three other children and a husband who were all suffering. I didn't know how to help them—or myself.

Just a few years earlier, I'd been a humor writer. I was on the staff of an internet startup, Wholefamily.com, that offered online counseling and articles on family wellness, as well as online plays that dramatized tough family situations like telling your kids you were getting divorced. I wrote the humor column, *Under Sherri's Hat*, a series of lighthearted observations on family life.

One called *Babysitter Blues* started like this: *I hate rejection. Rejection is painful. Especially rejection by 14-year-old girls. Especially when you're a 42-year-old woman dying to escape your four children… and you have to hear from another 14-year-old babysitter because her social life is more packed than Jennifer Aniston's.*

That had been the extent of my problems. Such wonderful ordinary everyday problems.

If you had seen me a few years after Koby's murder, you would have assumed that I was doing well. In order to stay alive for our other kids, for ourselves, and to honor Koby and Yosef, in 2002, we created a sleepaway camp for bereaved Israeli children. Thousands of children have attended Camp Koby.

I also wrote a memoir, *The Blessing of a Broken Heart*. I wrote about the way that my husband and I were able to take the cruelty of our son's murder and turn it into kindness through the work of the Koby Mandell Foundation.

My husband Seth and I became public exemplars of resilience, of transforming tragedy into transcendence. We were honored at dinners and won awards: the American Defamation League's Partners in Peace Award in Washington D.C., for example. I sat next to the baseball player Cal Ripken, Koby's hero, at a gala when he was honored by the Koby Mandell Foundation.

My book was adapted into a play that opened at the University of San Diego Repertory Theater. The book was translated into three languages. My husband and I spoke around the world—London, Hong Kong, Mexico City, all across America.

But that was the public me, the one on the stage. The one who was frantic to prove that she was okay. The one who spoke and wrote in a voice of triumph. The private me was different.

The private me longed for comfort. And I knew it wasn't going to be easy to find. Because once you have dwelled with Hades, once you have eaten the seeds of the pomegranate that grows in the underworld, it's hard to return to the land of light.

Your eyes have a difficult time adjusting. You can't describe what you witnessed there: few will understand. You have learned, for example, about Cerberus, the three-headed dog, who guards those in the underworld from leaving. You have seen his tail: that of a serpent. You know how he growls and bares his teeth, yet you know how to pet him, to stroke him under the belly so that he folds his legs, lies down and allows you to leave when you want.

Even though you have the ability to exit the underworld, you are not sure you want to. In fact, you no longer know which world you belong in or which world you prefer. The ordinary world is no longer hospitable in some ways: it's too light, too trivial. The underworld has the gravity, the shock, the darkness, the weight of being you crave.

I wanted to be a pastoral counselor because I needed to dwell in the underworld of the hospital. I wanted to help the people there, and I needed training to help the children and families I worked with through the Koby Mandell Foundation. But I knew it was really me who needed help. Because I had another dream: I hoped that I would meet a guide there who would reveal to me the secret of how to emerge from the darkness. I knew she or he could be anywhere: a patient, worker, visitor, doctor or a fellow student. Someone like the 36, the righteous of the generation, modest and inconspicuous.

The legend of the 36 says that there are 36 people who are so holy and so beautiful and special that it is because of them that the world continues to exist. They are present in every generation. And yet, they themselves don't know that they are a part of this fraternity.

They are so humble that they would never believe themselves to be part of an elevated community whose goodness sustains the world. Without the 36, it is said, the world would come to an end.

I imagined that this guide would tell me something so profound that all at once, everything would change. I would stop looking into the darkness for sustenance. I would leave death behind and once again I would take pleasure in the light and the fresh air.

Chapter 4

Class

I could never find a parking spot at the hospital; the lot was so crowded. It felt like a symbol of my situation as a pastoral counseling intern. It was hard for me to find my place in the hospital.

Pastoral counseling was a new field in Israel, so patients didn't understand what I was doing in their rooms. It's no surprise that most patients didn't welcome me or want my help. I imagined that they could sense my discomfort.

That day, I parked on the street and had to walk for twenty minutes uphill to the parking lot, past the strange looking two-story cream-colored smokestack that was part of the hospital. Sometimes a grey cloud of smoke burst forth from the chimney. What required so much burning? The scene was unsettling, especially in Jerusalem, with the chimney a painful reminder of the Holocaust.

As I walked down the hall to the pastoral counseling seminar, I looked into a room with an open door. An Arab woman sat in a chair, her head covered by a burgundy *hijab*, while her husband lay in bed with a black and white *keffiyeh* around his head.

At my first interview for the pastoral counseling course, my teacher, Michael, had told me that there were many Arab patients in the hospital. He asked me if, given the murder of my son, I would be able to work with Arab patients. I said I didn't know. I really didn't. "At your own pace," he said. "When you feel that it's right for you. When you're ready. And if not, we respect your decision."

I didn't hate Arabs. But I hated the ones who had killed my son. What would it feel like for me to walk into that room now? The second *intifada* had just ended. Thousands of Israelis and Palestinians had been killed. I didn't have a great desire to reach out to a Palestinian; in fact, in many ways, I dreaded it. But I wondered if talking to an Arab patient could ease my pain, provide a sense of comfort, for them and for me.

I walked into our classroom and Michael passed me a worksheet.

Class schedule November 19th
8:50 — Arrival and getting organized
9:00 — Deep breathing
9:10 — Opening blessings and text
9:20 — Sharing
Break
10:00 — Transcripts of students' hospital visits to patients
11:30 — Discussion of visiting the sick in the Bible
12:30 — Meeting with the head nurse of the oncology ward
1:00 — Lunch
Homework: Read Prayer and Presence

In the small conference room on the seventh floor, we sang a blessing for healing: "He who blessed our ancestors, Abraham, Isaac and Jacob, Sara, Rebecca, Rachel, and Leah, please bless and heal the one who is ill"—the same prayer for healing said in the synagogue each Sabbath.

We each named the patients we counseled in the hospital and people we knew personally who were sick, first their name and then their mother's name. We asked God to heal them. I felt that these blessings were useless. Why would God ever listen to us? Still I added my mother's name, Marilyn, the daughter of Edna. She had pain in her shoulders and legs, trouble walking. She lived far away in Florida, but I spoke to her a lot on the phone.

My mother had long ago been a cheerleader at Taft High School in the Bronx and in many ways, she was my cheerleader. She usually encouraged me. But when I told her that I was going to be working in the hospital she said, "Why become a pastoral counselor? I don't think it's a good idea to bring more suffering into your life. You've had enough pain."

"I need to learn something," I answered. "To help people."

"You already help people. Why would you do this? You don't need it."

And now, as we sang the blessings in class, I wondered if my mother was right. I felt so awkward, like an outsider and even worse, an imposter. The sweet singing of the others depressed me. My singing felt forced, unnatural. I couldn't find the right key. Everybody was singing together, gracefully, easily, their faces open, shining. The timbre of my voice was thin and weak.

I knew that Michael sang to patients in English and in Hebrew. I had once witnessed him singing to a patient in Russian. At our initial interview, he had asked me if I would sing to patients. He said that it was an excellent way to bond with the sick. But I am not a singer. There was no way I could imagine myself singing to a patient. How could I sing in all of this sorrow?

Still I had a fantasy that this year in the hospital, I would learn to relax, to breathe, to meditate—even to sing. My voice would become powerful. I would learn to meditate in order to calm myself. I would become a bold person who was free of all the anxiety that I was burdened with. I would become a transcendent loving being. I would work with Arab patients. I would radiate peace. I would wear white. I would know when to be silent. I would learn to be present. I would become somebody else.

Now Ora spoke in her soft musical voice. Her voice had an airy sweetness to it, like water cascading over a bed of stones: *Close your eyes. Root yourselves in the ground, empty your minds, let your breathing slow.* I peeked around the table, everyone else's eyes were closed. I wanted to be able to let go but I couldn't. I disliked guided imagery and breathing. Told to relax, I got tense. My mind shouted: *I don't want to relax.*

Instead I thought of what I needed to do for the kids: be home by 3:10, make them a snack of pita and melted cheese, unpack the dry goods from the grocery store that I had left in the car, drink a cup of tea, put in a load of laundry, make dinner. I opened my eyes. I took out my pen and made a grocery list. I waited.

We read a text from the Talmud about great rabbis who could not bear their own suffering. We learned a midrash about the death of Moses, how when God told him of his impending death, Moses argued with God to keep him alive.

Later, Varda, one of the students, talked about a visit she had made to a deaf man. "At first, he didn't look at me, his son was deaf too and he was there as well. I just smiled at them. I stood at the side of the bed. Then I took his hand. We held hands for maybe five minutes. It was like a prayer. I felt love, and when I walked out, he sent me a kiss in the air."

A kiss in the air. On my last visit, I'd been asked to leave!

At 1:00 P.M. the other students took out the food they had brought for our potluck lunch: hummus, pita, eggplant salad, tomatoes and cucumbers, hard boiled eggs, and olives. I took a few bites and as they chatted with each other, smiling and laughing. I walked away and down the corridor, downstairs for a coffee. I waited on line and wondered what the hell I was doing here.

The next day, I was back in the hospital to counsel patients. I walked through the lobby and past the oncology day center, a large room whose five-foot-high frosted glass wall fronted the hallway. The dozen black leather reclining armchairs were all taken—poison administered in the hope of healing. I continued down the dark corridor.

Room 7564. Reuven looked worn out, weak, emaciated, as if he had no power, as if he had never had any power. That's the thing with sick people: it's hard to imagine them well, physically hardy. I felt it so strongly here, the two different worlds: the land of the sick and the land of the well. The sick lived in a horizontal universe, lying in bed, while the rest of us strode by purposefully, still belonging to the world of the vertical, the upright, at least in terms of posture.

He lay in bed propped up in a sitting position, the faded blue hospital issue shirt with its pattern of overlapping hexagonal Jewish stars was rumpled; the strings hung untied, exposing a few curls of sparse white hair on his chest.

I knew Reuven was 55 from the information sheet that also listed his room number, bed number, age, date of hospitalization, dietetic restrictions, level of disability, identity number, and hospital identity number. The sheet told me that there were 23 beds on the cancer ward and today there were zero free hospital beds.

After I introduced myself, Reuven began to speak in a soft voice. He told me that he was an American citizen because his father had gone to Chicago to get a PhD, and he was born there. The family had returned to Israel when Reuven was ten.

After his service in the Israeli army, he had traveled in America and then stayed there for 23 years. Now he had finally returned to Israel. "These days, my biggest problem is keeping weight on. I'm not eating enough. So they're feeding me through this tube. But as soon as I get home, I'm going to work."

"What do you do?"

"I've had a whole lot of jobs. But right before I got sick, I was a deep-sea diver. I love going under the water. It's a whole different world down there. Our last trip was in Caesarea. There's supposed to be some ruins of shipwrecks there, and we heard that there might be gold. We saw beautiful fish. But we never found the treasure. Maybe one day I can dive again. You know nobody on this earth knows what will happen the next day. We are all going to die. I try to keep living the best way I can."

"Is it hard to do?"

He shook his head. "We are all going to die."

I didn't know what to say. Now that I am a trained pastoral counselor, I would probably ask him what those sentences meant to him. *We are all going to die. I try to keep living the best I can.* To return those sentences to him. How do you live the best you can? How do any of us? But then, I didn't have the courage or the skill to ask him about his acceptance of death and his will to keep living. To ask him if he worried about dying. To repeat: *Nobody knows what will happen the next day.* To ask if that scared him. To ask how he kept living well.

A guest lecturer once told us: "Patients say things sometimes, and those statements can be thought of as burning bushes—like the one in the Bible. Important sentences that shimmer and even flame and never stop burning. That stop us in our tracks. Those are the sentences that we need to pause for and respect.

"Like Moses stopped at the burning bush. Other shepherds were in the area that day, but nobody stopped to notice. Moses did. God told him to take off his shoes because he was standing on holy ground. And the bush burned but it was not consumed.

"There are traumas in our lives that will always keep on burning. But when you notice them and when you talk to a patient and you have that kind of intimacy and truth, it's as if you are standing on holy ground."

I was there in the hospital to stand on this holy ground. But I didn't know how to approach those burning bushes. I wasn't ready. I was timid, afraid of hurting Reuven with a question he wasn't ready to hear. Or maybe I wasn't ready for the answer.

It's not surprising that Reuven changed the subject. "Can you help me out of this bed?"

I stood next to the bed, gave him my hand and held his bony fingers as I pulled his weight toward me, and he slowly swung his legs over the bed. I handed him his brown furry slippers and he slipped them on and stood on the floor. I held his hand as he shuffled across the floor and into the orange arm chair in the corner of the room. Once he was settled, I asked, "Are you comfortable?"

"Oh yes," he said.

I wondered if he had anybody caring for him. "Are you married?" I asked.

"It's a long story," he said, running his fingers over his scalp, scrunching up his shoulders and releasing them. "One year I worked as a guide on rafting expeditions. I spent all of my time on the Colorado River. Wonderful. Have you ever been there? You should go there. But after that, well, I got married. We had five children. They're all still in America. I became the co-owner of a restaurant, a chain. I owned four restaurants in Atlanta. We made good money but one year, the CFO asked me to sign a document, and I didn't think much of it."

He coughed, hacking so hard it sounded like his body was

turning inside out. His face turned red and he extracted a crumpled tissue from the cuff of his pajamas and spit into it. Then he took a deep breath. It was a minute before he could speak again.

"He said he needed my signature before the end of the year, or the company would lose money. Well, this guy was up to something because the next week, they told me there was an accounting discrepancy.

"Some discrepancy. To the tune of half a million dollars. I had to take the fallout because I'd signed the paper. It was innocent on my part, but let me tell you, I got framed. They took me to prison and within a year, my wife divorced me."

He spoke quietly, gently. I had to listen very closely to hear him. I no longer saw the medical apparatus in the room or heard the beeping of the oxygen machines around us. I saw only Reuven.

"The judge hardly gave me a trial, I mean there was no jury. It was the accountant's word against mine. They took me to the worst prison. Where they jail murderers and rapists. The first night they came to fight me, I broke three guys' shoulders—I'm a master in *krav maga*. After that, they wanted to move me to another prison. I was bound up with ropes and lying on the bed of the truck, because they thought I was a dangerous criminal." He smiled and wiped his mouth with the back of his hand, cupped his hand on his chin and looked at me.

I wondered if maybe he was high on painkillers or morphine and he was making this whole story up. "What a story," I said.

"I'm a black belt, ninth Dan. The highest level. I learned it in the IDF. Self-defense." He smiled and coughed again. "Too bad my knees gave out when I turned forty."

Could it be true I wondered? Ninth Dan. Whatever it was, it sounded impressive. He looked emaciated, frail. Maybe he was hallucinating. Surely he was exaggerating. But it wasn't my job to disbelieve or question or judge. At least I didn't think it was.

"Later I taught *krav maga* in South Korea."

I remembered my father going mad when he was dying. Nine years earlier, my father had died at the age of 74 from cancer of the thymus gland. He got sick at the same time that my family and I moved from Silver Spring, Maryland to Israel. We didn't know he had cancer that August when we boarded the plane to make *aliyah*, only that he was losing weight and was coughing. In fact, he was a little proud of his thinner physique.

Five months later, I traveled from Israel to Delray Beach, Florida to help take care of him. He'd been operated on and the doctor said that the operation was a success, but I could see that my father had not recovered. He couldn't eat and weighed less than I did. And he had been a big man. Only the visiting nurse warned me that he was near death.

A few days later he was readmitted to a hospital in Boca Raton. I visited him on Saturday night. The halls were quiet, and the ward felt as if the staff had deserted it, like an abandoned town. He looked like a little boy in a large bed, he had shrunk down so much. He lay there, his beautiful hair now thin, his large hands now looked like bones without flesh, and he said that I had to leave, that I would miss my plane even though I was not flying anywhere that night. He kept insisting that I leave. Instead it was he who was leaving us.

Now I asked Reuven: "I wonder if you see cancer as a fight, like the one you had in the prison."

"Cancer is also a fight, but it's not with the disease. I mean with this disease, the kind I have, there's only one ending. The fight is with the pain. I fight the pain. If I'm too doped up," he said, "it's like I'm not in this world."

"I know," I said, thinking about my son. The pain kept me connected to him. It was a reminder of all we had lost. But I didn't say anything about that. Instead I said, "I know what you mean, when I gave birth to my youngest, after three natural births, I had an epidural and I felt that I was watching myself give birth. I didn't feel the pain, but I didn't feel the joy. I was removed from the experience."

"Yes, pain sometimes tells us we are alive," he said.

I nodded my head.

"After that night, I was taken to another prison," he continued. "And I had to fight some more. A gang of lowlifes came after me and I fought them off. One black guy, well I put my belt on the bed and told him it was a snake. That worked. He believed in magic. After that night, they didn't touch me.

"They came to me with their problems. I wrote letters for them and researched their cases. I was the jailhouse lawyer. I helped them. I don't mean to be prejudiced but some of those people, well they have only a fifth-grade education."

I didn't know whether or not to believe this story. Maybe it was the drugs. Or maybe it was true. I looked into his eyes. He looked straight back at me. There was strength, determination, power. I told him that he reminded me of Joseph in the Bible who survived prison by interpreting dreams.

"I managed yes, but I was in prison for too long a time."

There was silence. I didn't know what to say. I was there to be a pastoral counselor, to say something spiritual. I asked: "Do you see the soul as some kind of treasure?"

Reuven laughed. "Maybe the soul is a treasure. I don't know… But God is here with me. He's not up in the sky. I see God as part of me and me as part of God."

I was wondering how to respond when the nurse entered and asked him about his bowel movements. It was a perfect time to excuse myself.

The next week I wrote up a transcript about the meeting and we discussed it in class. We sat around the conference table, our books and notebooks scattered on the table. The fluorescent light hummed. Somebody had written a list of patients' names on a whiteboard in the corner, presumably for a staff meeting. I passed out the three-page record of our conversation and two of the students read the passage aloud to the class, as if it were a script.

"Comments?" asked Ora.

Ruth closed her eyes before she spoke. She tilted her head and asked me: "When you talk about the pain of labor, is that a valid comparison?"

"Can you really feel what he is feeling, and don't you hurt him by saying that? I don't think you can feel what he feels," said Michael.

"It sounds as if you were comparing morphine and cancer to an epidural and birth," said Ora. "Is that what you want to do?"

My teachers and classmates disapproved. And I wondered, maybe I shouldn't have told Reuven that I knew how he felt. The pain of childbirth and the pain of dying of cancer are not commensurate.

I hadn't felt that I had hurt him. But now I felt terrible. Maybe I had been like all those people who had come to me after Koby's murder and said exactly the wrong thing.

Chapter 5

A Voice of Comfort

In class we were asked to write our professional goals. I wrote:
To be able to help those who suffer.
To understand my own suffering and how I can use it to help others.
To be able to pray.
Michael asked us, "Do you know about the Physician's Prayer by Maimonides? It might be good to say before your visits. It helps to start your visit with a prayer, an intention." Michael grew up in Brooklyn and had a strong American accent so when he spoke Hebrew it was easy for me to understand him.

Maimonides is the twelfth century rabbi and scholar whose commentaries and books like *A Guide to the Perplexed* and the *Mishnah Torah* are still studied. Not only a brilliant and accomplished philosopher, he was also the personal physician to Saladin, the powerful ruler of Egypt.

Maimonides excelled in disciplines ranging from law to astronomy. He worked tirelessly, treating patients into the evenings, yet also wrote treatises and books on everything from the world-to-come to hemorrhoids.

Michael read part of the prayer:
Almighty God, you have created the human body with infinite wis-

dom.

In your eternal providence, you have chosen me to watch over the life and health of your creation.
I am now about to apply myself to the duties of my profession.
Support me in these great labors that they may benefit humankind.
For without your help, not even the least thing will succeed…
Preserve the strength of my body and soul
that they may ever be ready to help
rich and poor, good and bad, enemy as well as friend.
In the sufferer let me see only the human being. (adapted by Rabbi Simcha Weintraub)

The language of this prayer, at least in its translation, didn't speak to me. I wasn't a physician. I didn't believe that I had great labors in the hospital. I didn't pay any attention then to the call in the prayer to help enemy as well as friend, though I'd been debating my own ability to do just that. I was naïve about the physical and spiritual toll of being so close to suffering because I was too preoccupied with my own pain. Yet I didn't talk about it.

Only once in class had I shared my story of Koby, and that was when I was given 15 minutes to introduce myself. I knew that I shouldn't talk about myself with the patients. Yet Koby's murder accompanied me in class and on all of my visits. Almost every conversation rubbed against my own wounds. Sometimes after a visit to a patient, I would feel weak and need to sit down.

As far as turning to God, though I was willing to talk to the divine in my own words, I felt far away from God. I hadn't learned to pray as a child, so the words of the formal prayers usually felt foreign in my mouth. I'd never gone to temple as a kid, never gone to Sunday School or Hebrew school. My father didn't like the temple; he said that it was a fashion show.

In 1968, the year that my friends all celebrated their bar and bat mitzvahs, I didn't have one. Still I spent many Saturday mornings with my friends—Jane and Karen and Claudia and Debbie—at the Hewlett-East Rockaway Jewish Center on Main Street, not far from my home. Some of my friends would escape from the sanctuary, and during services, we lounged on the green vinyl couch in the large ladies' room where a huge mirror hung over the long linoleum counter that ran the length of the room.

There we rummaged through the remains of the basket of toiletries left over from the previous week's wedding: White Mist hairspray, Bonne Belle eye shadow, tampons, St. Joseph's aspirin, Ban spray-on deodorant, Revlon nail polish, Mini Mist dry shampoo, a small sewing kit. My friends and I sampled the goodies, laughing as we sprayed our hair and polished our nails bright red. The room filled with an astringent cloud of deodorant spray and nail polish remover fumes.

Later we took turns lying on the stained olive-green carpet of the inner bridal dressing room. We stationed ourselves around one girl's body, one girl at her head, two on either side of her legs and another two on opposite sides of her torso. We each tucked two fingers underneath her, our palms facing up. We concentrated, focusing all of our mental energy toward lifting the girl from the floor, so that she would levitate effortlessly, hovering over our open hands.

But the girl never rose in our hands, no lifting of the burden of matter ever occurred. Afterwards, my friends returned to their parents waiting for them in the sanctuary, and I walked the few blocks home, glad to be released from the starched atmosphere of the temple where everybody read from a prayer book whose alternating pages were printed in a language I didn't know.

Yet after Koby was killed, something in me needed the language of prayer. The words of the formal prayers—the morning blessings, the *Shema*, and the Psalms were written in an exalted language that I longed for: pure, rich words that spoke of suffering and redemption.

Ordinary words didn't suffice. We had been kicked out of the realm of the ordinary. I needed holy words that transcended the limits of this world. I needed to believe that I would be reunited with my son as stated in the Eighteen Blessings. "He sustains the living with kindness, resuscitates the dead with abundant mercy…"

Of course I had no idea how I would ever see Koby again. Would I hug him again? Talk to him? Doubtful. Still I needed to believe that I would be reunited with him in some way. The words of the prayer gave me hope.

More recently though, I didn't enter prayer, or the words didn't enter me. They lay at my feet like rocks that were too heavy to lift. What was the point? I didn't feel that God changed his plans based on our prayers. I felt betrayed: How could he allow such suffering in the world? Part of me wanted to talk to God but part of me suspected that he didn't care.

A few minutes later, Ora looked around the room and said: *I'd like you all to do a writing exercise. If you were sick who could comfort you? Who would be your ideal visitor? What would he or she look like? What would they say?*

Who would be the one to comfort me? I looked at my fellow students who were already writing as if the task were no problem for them. Jacob was a Buddhist whose head was shaved like a monk's. Varda was a social worker with a beautiful singing voice. One student worked as a gardener and another as a nursery school teacher.

Almost all of us were there because we knew suffering: the loss of a father or mother, or a child, or a sister. Illness. The need to care for a sick mother, or an alcoholic father.

I didn't want to imagine myself sick or suffering. I was afraid of calling more suffering to myself, so at first I didn't write. But I was an obedient student and because I had suffered and experienced comfort, I imagined who might help me:

I hear footsteps.

I want someone with an open face.

Someone with big hands who is not afraid—older than me.

She comes in and stands without speaking. She takes my hand; her hand is dry. "How did you sleep?" she asks. She strokes my hands. She stands straight, and looks me in the eyes.

I needed somebody without fear. I needed a kind and compassionate mother, like my own. Until my mother was 75, she was in good health. Now she had a problem with her hip and shoulder—she had had an operation on her rotator cuff a few years earlier, but it didn't help. And because of the pains and weakness in her arms and legs, she found it difficult to walk or to lift things. She couldn't take out her own garbage, she couldn't cook.

She had help at her home in Delray Beach, Florida, a woman from the island of Jamaica named Verona who came to her home each morning, and sometimes on a hard day, stayed the afternoon as well. When I visited my mom the previous March, we went to her doctor and he took me aside and told me that she would most likely deteriorate further, that she might not be able to stay in her own home. That she could die.

She was fading but she was still enjoying life. In fact, after my father died, she found a boyfriend who was younger than me—in his early 40s. She met Rafael at the library. He worked as an addiction counselor in the local prison.

I really didn't know what to think about their relationship, other than to be a little proud but also suspicious. If he thought she had money, he was sadly mistaken.

When I visited my mother in Florida and he was around, she didn't complain at all. She watched TV with him, they chatted, and they laughed. He even helped her dye her hair. When he was around, she wasn't sick.

But last week on the phone she told me that she wanted her mother. (My grandmother had been dead for 30 years.) And then yesterday, she told me she had been praying. My mother was not a woman who prayed—she wasn't at all religious—but painkillers and pain had pushed her to pray. She told me that she'd been praying to God. Only God was her mother.

A year before Koby was murdered, when our dog Sibyl had puppies, we gave one of them to our neighbor, an old Sephardic lady who began life in a faraway Arab country. The puppy kept digging her way under the fence that separated our yards, returning to us. Our neighbor finally gave the puppy back, saying: *Everybody wants their mother.*

It seemed that so many people wanted a mother when they were sick. I could hear it on the ward, sick people calling out *Ima, Mama, mommy,* or more rarely *Abba, Daddy.* The thin, rattling voices sighing, moaning for a parent—no matter how old they were or how long their parents had been dead. There is something within many of us that longs for the comfort of our mother or father.

After Koby was killed, Moshe Katzav, the president of Israel, came to our house. I told him: *I need a father, an Abba.* He didn't respond. He looked at me with his lips pressed together but he didn't smile. He had grey hair and dark eyes, olive skin, a pleasant face, but he didn't reach out to me. He didn't say a word. I wanted

Katzav to act like a father with me, even though he wasn't that much older than I was. (This was before his forced resignation and trial and imprisonment because he was found guilty of rape.)

My own father was dead. What I meant was that I needed somebody to comfort me, to give me the shelter of his being, somebody to give me faith that I would survive.

Later I was embarrassed that I had spoken to him like that. But I could hear it on the ward—people calling out to their parents, crying for comfort. People begging for somebody to love them and nurture them and stay with them and take care of them. When we are in pain, it's hard not to feel like a child longing for protection.

I hear footsteps.

I want someone with an open face…

Someone with big hands who is not afraid—older than me.

She comes in and stands without speaking. She takes my hand. Her hand is dry. "How did you sleep?" she asks. She strokes my hands. She stands straight and looks me in the eyes.

Then she says, "I am not going to leave you. I will stay here by your side."

Chapter 6

Cooking Without Fire

The etymology of the word *patient* is to undergo, to suffer, to bear, from the Latin. But it seemed to me that Reuven refused to be defined by suffering. Michael told me that from his hospital bed, Reuven was calling friends, asking to borrow a computer that they weren't using so that he could play games online.

When he saw me on the threshold of his room that grey afternoon, Reuven smiled and opened his hands toward me. "Come in," he said, as if he were a gentleman inviting me to his afternoon tea party in a manor house. "Would you like some Constant Comment?" He leaned over from his bed and slid open the top drawer of his white plastic night table and showed me his stash of tea, arrayed there in a row of boxes. "My niece brought me some special teas." A gray plastic electric kettle sat on the counter above the white sink opposite the bed.

"Try some," he said.

I shook my head. I couldn't eat or drink in a hospital room.

When I was in seventh grade, my sister and I used to volunteer on Friday afternoons as candy stripers at St. Joseph's Hospital in Far Rockaway, bringing patients their meals on trays. I loved my red and white striped bib jumper uniform. I liked the rattle of the cart as I pushed it down the linoleum floors, the smiles of the patients when they saw me, even my name tag. But at the end of my shift, when I left the hospital, I was nauseous, unable to eat. The hospital smell clung to me. I still felt sick to my stomach on these wards.

"Nothing is passing through me," Reuven said. "I'm all stopped up. Constipated. It's because of the cancer medication. I came on the bus, and they're giving me a laxative. I don't have a car, and I can't take the bus home to Beit Shemesh. I told the doctor it could be risky for me to be on the bus," he said giggling, wiping his mouth with his hand. "If you know what I mean."

I nodded. I looked at Reuven and he reminded me a little of my father, the way his eyes were magnified in his glasses. He opened the drawer of his metal hospital night table and offered me miniature Milky Ways, Mars Bars, chocolate kisses. "Won't you have some?" he asked, like a Southern gentleman. I shook my head no. "Are you sure you won't have a cup of tea?"

"No thank you."

A thin tube was taped to Reuven's forehead, a junction of three crosses of white strips. A horn of plastic emerged from his head, as if he'd become a mythic unicorn. I'm not sure if he was being fed through his forehead, but something was going through there.

A plastic bag, quart size, like a zip lock bag used to store food, hung from the bottom of his hospital bed bulging with drippings from his body, spinach colored. He said, "Don't mind the bag. It's just from this Diet Coke. And the other things I'm drinking."

"It's fine," I said but I was not going to look in that direction.

"If you don't like Constant Comment, I also have Wissotzky."

I told him no. "Can you eat anything?" I asked.

"Not for the moment."

I wondered how long that moment would be.

A pair of white plastic gloves lay flat on the bottom of the plastic garbage pail next to the chair where I sat.

"I can't even eat rice," he said, taking off his glasses which looked enormous on his thin emaciated face, wiping them with the hem of the hospital sheet. "Most people don't understand rice," he said. "Rice has a taste all of its own and shouldn't be covered with sauce. Most people put too much spice on it. You have to taste the taste of the rice."

"My rice never turns out well," I admitted.

"How do you cook it?" he asked.

"I do a ratio of two to one," I said. "But it's always sticky."

His face suddenly turned red and he spit into a tissue. He took a series of shallow breaths and then he began to cough. Alarmed that he was choking, I got up to call a nurse, but he raised one finger to me and shook his head no. I waited. It took a long while till he could speak again.

"Here's what you do," he said. "You put in about a finger's worth of rice, two fingers worth of water." He coughed and coughed, covering his mouth with a handkerchief he grabbed from his night table. I waited for him to stop.

"Are you okay?"

"Yes."

"I don't know how to measure like that," I said. "I always wondered what they meant by a finger."

I heard the sound of an alarm coming from another room. Nobody seemed to be hurrying to turn it off. "A finger is like a shot, a percentage of a bottle, a thirtieth of a bottle…you need 30 of them to use up the entire bottle. Did I tell you that I used to be a bartender?" Reuven always seemed to surprise me. He coughed. "More important…there is something lovely you can do with rice. I mean not everybody likes it plain. Do you like curry?" he asked.

"I like it, but I don't know how to make it."

"Use Bombay curry," he said. "It shouldn't be too yellow, too dark, and it shouldn't have too much turmeric. Don't buy that one. You can mix the curry with an all in one spice, and then with some oil—a few tablespoons. You cook some eggplant in water, and you make a sauce, not with tomato, just eggplant and water, and you keep cooking the eggplant until it dissolves.

"Then you add the curry. It's so tasty. Mix it with some lamb—you can get neck of lamb —it's not too expensive, go to the market in the center of Jerusalem, Machane Yehuda, and ask them for it.

"The next day, after the meat is gone take what's left of the curry—even if there's no meat left, just the sauce, and sop it up with bread. That's all you need for a wonderful meal, just that leftover curry."

He was hollowed out, his pajamas hung on him. He had only a scruff of a beard. His calves were thin and hairless. He hadn't eaten, might never eat again, and yet we were enjoying his recipe. "That sounds wonderful," I said.

I heard coughing from the next bed, the shuffle of feet.

What should I say now? Should I talk about loss, the loss of appetite, the loss of food in his life? No, I didn't have to speak. I had learned from Ora that a big part of our job was the ability to be silent. Not feeling that we had to fill the air with conversation. Besides, I had to leave; my son Gavi would be home from school soon, and I wanted to be with him for lunch, I wanted to make him something to eat—a toasted cheese sandwich, plain, unexceptional. Yet I was of two minds: part of me was racing home. But part of me wanted to stay and speak with Reuven about the spicy burning curry.

He said, "Oh, I forgot to tell you that you can add a bay leaf. They grow all over this area—on trees."

"I never saw them."

"You have to look for them. They're all over. When I get out of here, I'll show you. Or just ask somebody who knows trees, botany."

We were drawing a circle around the illness, surrounding it with a pungent taste and penetrating aroma. We were sharing a meal, purging the hospital room of its antiseptic monotony. "Look," I said pointing, "your hospital door is the color of turmeric."

He smiled.

When I left the room, I said: "I hope that one day I will be blessed to eat food that you prepare."

He said, "I hope so too."

On my way home I stopped to buy eggplant. I wanted to eat only spicy. I wanted to live in a world that was savory and seasoned and dripping with life. I wanted to dip my bread in all of it.

Chapter 7

A Mistake

The first time I visited Rena, a 67-year-old woman with lung cancer, she was so still I was afraid that she was dead. I hurried to call a nurse—I didn't want to be the one to find a dead person—but before I left the room, she cleared her throat.

Then she began coughing. I brought her a paper towel from the dispenser next to the sink. I felt like gagging when she spit into the towel. I closed my eyes and breathed. I felt weak and dizzy. My head hurt.

Rena coughed some more. I brought her water, held the plastic cup close to her mouth to make it easier for her to sip through a straw. She stopped coughing and breathed in a great gulp of air.

Rena had smooth olive skin and thin hair, large hazel eyes. Her face had a sheen of sweat on it and her eyes were heavily hooded. A needle was taped to her hand. The air smelled like yeast and sour bread.

I introduced myself, told Rena that I was a pastoral counselor. She didn't know what that was, so I told her that spiritual care meant trying to help people find some greater meaning in life. She smiled. "It's fine for you to be here," she said.

I didn't know what to say but that week in class we had studied a Psalm. We learned that King David wrote the Psalms when he was inspired by the spirit of God and for that reason the Psalms are supposed to be healing. I wasn't so sure, but I figured I would give it a try.

Even though I wasn't very familiar with the Psalms, I asked her softly, "Would you like me to read you a Psalm?"

Yes, she whispered.

My reading in Hebrew wasn't great so I read very slowly, trying to enunciate each word:

I look to the hills; from where will my help come?
Let my help come from God
Who shapes heaven and earth
May he not permit your foot to waver
May your protector not slumber
Behold the keeper of Israel neither slumbers nor sleeps
If the Lord is your protector
If the Lord is your shade at your right hand
The sun will not harm you by day and there will be a moon at night
The Lord will guard you from all evil; he will guard your soul
The Lord will preserve your going out and your homecoming from this time forth and for all the future.

The Psalms have difficult Hebrew; even Hebrew speakers have a hard time understanding the words, so it didn't surprise me that I stumbled over them. As I read, Rena closed her eyes and said the words with me. *May your protector not slumber. Behold the keeper of Israel neither slumbers nor sleeps.*

I was trying hard to read the words correctly. She closed her eyes and cried. I waited. Then I read again. She opened her eyes and again mouthed the words along with me. She began to correct my pronunciation. She laughed at me. "American, huh?" she said. "You have a really strong accent." She kept laughing and wiped her eyes with the tissue. She corrected another word I mispronounced. Then she closed her eyes and said the Psalm by heart, slowly, word by word in a whisper. It felt to me as if her body, though weak and fragile, had become a prayer. She opened her eyes and smiled at me when she finished. Her reading was more moving than any theater performance I had ever witnessed. I asked her, "How do you know the Psalms so well?"

"I learned them fifty years ago. I was home sick for a few months. I kept reading the Psalms. I don't know why but that's what I did. Once I was a very pious girl. Nobody could believe that I had memorized them all. I can say them all by heart." She looked up at me and nodded. I began reading another Psalm. She said, "Just keep reading," and she closed her eyes and whispered the words along with me.

The next week when I went into Rena's room, a young man and a young woman stood next to the radiator; they looked like they were in their thirties. It was late December and very cold. The radiator burst forth with staccato sounds and then was silent. The two were tall and thin, built like runners. Though they had different coloring, I was sure they were brother and sister. The man had large hazel eyes, dark silky bangs brushed to the side of his forehead. He wore a pressed white shirt and black striped pants, a black crocheted yarmulke the size of a soup bowl on the back of his head. The woman had a thick tangle of long blonde hair in ringlets. She wore a long black sweater and a shirt that exposed her midriff.

Rena lay with her eyes closed. Dried spit caked the corners of her mouth. "Ima, wake up," the man said.

"It's okay, let her sleep," I said. "I'm Sherri, a pastoral counselor."

"My mother told us you'd been here to visit. Ima, somebody is here to see you."

"I don't want to bother her if she's asleep."

"No, it's fine," the woman said. "She needs to get up. She told us you were here, that you read Psalms together. She wanted to see you."

I walked up close to the bed and held Rena's hand. She opened her eyes and looked at me and then at her children. She began to laugh, and then to cry. The laughter sounded like tears and the crying sounded like laughter. I couldn't tell which was which.

Rena looked so sick and pale and wasted but her large eyes were such a beautiful color, like the brown-green color of the Atlantic Ocean, the sea of my childhood.

"You can speak English," the daughter said to me in perfect English.

"How do you know English so well?" I asked her.

"I live in Sydney," she said, putting her fingers over her mouth.

"That's really far away. What do you do there?"

"I'm a fashion designer."

"Do you miss Israel?" I asked.

"I've been in Australia for a long time." She handed her mother a tissue.

"How long has it been since you've been home?" I asked.

"Thirteen years. But you see I have this great younger brother, Avi," she said looking at her brother. "He helps our mother."

I was surprised. Why would she stay away for so long? Something beeped from the other side of the room. A nurse walked in and pushed a button on the device on the IV pole and the red numbers stopped flashing. She looked our way, pulled the curtain between the beds closed as if she were a stagehand in a play where the actors had finished Scene I. The nurse hurried off. Thirteen years is a long time to be away, I thought.

"You live in Jerusalem?" I asked Avi.

"Yes, in Gilo. I'm here a lot. Since my mother got sick nine months ago."

"Are there other kids?" I could hear a cart rattling the hallway, either lunch or laundry.

"We have another sister," said Avi. "But she doesn't come to visit."

Rena whimpered softly. She might have been laughing or crying. It was hard to tell. The daughter gave her a tissue and she held it to her eyes.

I told them: "I've heard that laughter and crying sometimes come from the same place. They aren't always opposites. There's a place where they merge."

"Ima, why are you crying?" the daughter asked. Rena shook her head and began to laugh. Tears poured from her eyes. And then she seemed to be sleeping.

"When my father was sick," I told the siblings, "I had to travel the opposite direction. We'd just moved to Israel, and my father was in Florida. He got cancer and I traveled from Israel to Delray Beach to be with him. He died seven years ago."

I thought of my father in the hospital in Florida, how he wanted the windows opened, how he would have liked to listen to the sea. And I remembered something suddenly. I told the siblings: "Before my father died, I was in the pool at my mother's retirement condo in Florida. Almost everybody there was elderly. But there were two younger men sitting on the edge of the pool. I dipped my feet in the water, on the side of the pool, and I was thinking about my father. The men came over to me and asked me what I was doing in the retirement community. I told them I was visiting because my father was very sick with cancer, and that he was in the hospital. One turned to me and said, "*Now is the time to tell your father how much you love him. Tell him it's okay for him to go. It will make his passing easier.*"

Those men were like angels, I thought to myself later, messengers sent to tell me what to do, to offer me wisdom. "Those men were the only ones, besides the visiting nurse, who told me that my father would die. I went to the hospital that day and told my father that I loved him. He died two weeks later when I was back in Israel." The siblings looked at me as if they didn't understand what I was talking about. Their mother opened her eyes.

Nobody uttered a word. I waited. I filled the silence. I turned to Rena: "Your kids are here because they love you."

Silence. Nobody spoke. I felt the pressure of silence. I had said the wrong thing, pushed too hard, forced things, done exactly what I should not have done.

I had blown it. In fact, just that week a psychiatrist had visited our class and explicitly told us that we were not supposed to introduce our own experiences into the pastoral conversations. We were to wait until the patient introduced a topic. I was supposed to listen, not to lead. How could I have said that? What was I possibly thinking? Why was I talking about my father?

I held my breath. I had made a mistake here. Silence.

Then Avi said, "You know, we're not like a normal family. Our parents are divorced. My father left us and he married somebody else and we don't have any contact with him. And my mother went out and had boyfriends. One stole her money. I don't know how he did it, but he got into her savings account. Maybe she let him. We never had Friday night dinner together. We don't have holidays together. We're not like those wonderful smiling Israeli families who are always visiting each other and happy together. My mother wasn't easy to get along with. That's why my sister isn't here."

How could I have talked about love? I felt so foolish.

Again silence. The mother began to laugh or cry or both. I couldn't tell.

Then the daughter from Sydney walked closer to the bed. "You know Ima, it's because of you I got my interest in fashion," she said, stroking her hand. "You always loved to get dressed so beautifully." She gently patted the tears from her mother's eyes with a tissue.

Avi walked closer to his mother and held her hand on the other side of the bed. They flanked her sides and they both held her hands. The daughter said: "You know she worked at the Cameri Theatre."

"What did she do?" I asked.

"She was in the box office. But I learned a lot from being there. I think I got my love of costumes there."

His sister smiled. "They let us take acting classes there, for free."

"And remember we went to those shows. That show with all that smoke—and the one with those gigantic puppets? Some of those shows we didn't understand a thing."

They laughed together.

"What do you do now?" I asked Avi.

"I was also influenced by my parents." Avi said. "My mother got such a lousy divorce settlement, I decided to study law at Hebrew University."

The mother opened her eyes, talked to me in halting English. "I speak English too," Rena said. "I learned it from Frank Sinatra—on the radio."

"She likes his songs," Avi said. They laughed.

"Ima," the daughter said, "thank you for everything you gave us."

They stood on either side of the bed, holding her hands. Avi cried softly, his head bent forward. He kissed his mother's hand.

The daughter took a tissue and wiped her own eyes. They said, "Thank you Ima, thank you."

Two weeks later I ran into the sister from Australia in a coffee shop in Jerusalem. She was carrying a tray to her table. I was on line to order.

"How is your mother?" I asked her.

"She died. But before my mother died, I convinced my sister to come from Eilat. She hadn't spoken to my mother in twelve years. She was so angry with her after she started having boyfriends. Especially after that one took the money. My sister couldn't forgive her. But she came, and we were all together for the first time. It was wonderful," he said.

It was a risk that day to talk about love. Maybe it was a mistake.

But there was love in the room with Rena and her children; I felt it woven into the pain of their sadness. Later I learned that sometimes the role of a pastoral counselor is to take a risk, to help expose the difficult places and deepen the pain, so that it can be shared. And I came to understand that deepening that pain can be a comfort.

Chapter 8

Looking the Wrong Way

My professional goals:
To have less anxiety
To use prayer to try to understand where the anxiety is coming from
To learn more about the Psalms

It was a cold and rainy January day. I shivered as I sat with Michael in his small windowless office. He stirred his tea, metal clinking against glass, and advised me to visit a woman named Vlada, who was not doing well.

He told me that she was all alone, a bereaved mother without any family. Her only son had died in an accident. I felt especially sad for her. After Koby's murder, my other children had saved me. I had to get up in the morning for them.

I walked down the hall to room 7362. Vlada lay in the bed next to the window, a white bandage wrapped around her scalp, an orange plastic cord draped over her ears, oxygen prongs in her nostrils.

A strong odor in the room reminded me of the dank water that remains in a vase after the dead flowers are discarded. But there were no flowers in this room. No photos or food or grandchildren's drawings as I saw in many other rooms, nothing on the bedside table but a plastic cup of water and a bright orange plastic pitcher. No hints of who the person was—or had been.

There were two other women in the room. One sat on an armchair in the far corner reading *Women's Housekeeping* in English. She wore a red-striped shirt and black trousers; a black headband held her long black straight hair off her forehead. She had prominent cheekbones, brown wide-spaced eyes. I introduced myself.

"I'm Helen," she said with an accent I couldn't place. "Vlada's aide."

"Where are you from?" I asked.

"Sri Lanka. I've been with the Madame for three years. I'm here every day," she said. "I don't leave her alone."

A tall thin woman with straight white hair in a bob sat on the end of the bed. She wore a black sweater jacket and baggy black trousers. Her skin was pale, and her deep-set eyes were pale blue. I introduced myself again and she said: "I can't stand to see Vlada like this. I can't stand it. There's nothing to do for her. Nothing. Look at her." Her voice was deep and gravelly, the voice of a smoker.

The hospital loudspeaker blared 100, 100, which I thought was the code for an emergency. But I didn't hear anybody hurrying anywhere. Vlada had no color in her face and her eyes were closed, her chest heaving. Helen kept reading her magazine.

The friend continued: "She's all hooked up. She's got a lot of tubes. Like our prime minister. She's in a coma." Ariel Sharon, the former prime minister, had been rushed to the hospital earlier in the week as the result of a stroke.

"Are you family?" I asked her.

"No, there is no family left." The pain of that sentence landed in my belly. "I'm her best friend. I wish I could do something, but there's nothing to do," said the woman with the white hair.

A barrage of hail sounded outside the window.

We stood and opened the curtain and looked outside. The landscape suddenly looked frozen, caked in white, and seemed to match the atmosphere in the room. "She's totally unresponsive. She's gone."

"I've read about people in comas," I said, "and they say that not all of the senses leave. Smell is the last thing to go. But sometimes, people in comas can still hear. I mean I'm not an expert. But I think some part of her can hear. You may be able to still speak to her."

I didn't know, but I hoped that it was true, that there was some communication possible. But the woman with white hair didn't turn to Vlada. She spoke to me: "She was so beautiful. So beautiful. And talented. And now she's so alone." She took out a tissue from her red leather purse and blew her nose.

"Have you known her a long time?"

"I knew her in Moscow before either of us were married. Vlada has known so much suffering. Her only son died when he was 22. Her only child. And it hurts me, there's no family here. She has a brother but he's in America. And her husband died. He had a stroke at home, and he never came out of it. But she managed to survive. She's a good woman. A fighter."

I wished that I had met Vlada earlier, so that we could have, perhaps, shared our stories, our sadness. "How did she manage?"

"I don't know—but she had a great spirit. She was very artistic. Their house was elegant, beautiful paintings all over the walls. She wasn't rich but she had exquisite taste."

"Were you with her, did you help her when her son died?"

"Yes. It was a bus accident. They were so close—her only child. It was so hard for Vlada. Naftali was traveling in India and it was a rainy night and the bus went off of the side of the road and he died. His girlfriend survived but she never even came to visit Vlada. Vlada had begged him not to go traveling in India. She had a bad feeling about it. But he went anyway. He was so young. Vlada always said that Naftali died for nothing, for nothing. So much loss and sadness. I was with her through all of that."

My stomach clenched. I didn't like the phrase: *dying for nothing*. I didn't want to think my son *died for nothing*. All of us want our lives to have mattered. To feel that we lived for something. I knew I shouldn't talk about myself, so I said nothing about the foundation my husband and I began in Koby's name, nothing about how hard we had worked to make his death matter.

I took a deep breath. "If you've been through that, you must be very close."

"We are. And now she's so alone. It hurts."

I could hear Helen turning the pages of her magazine. I looked at the hospital wall, the large photograph of bright red petunias that was probably chosen as a reminder of beauty and life. The picture seemed to be trying—and failing—to cheer us up. The friend spoke to Vlada: "Darling, you need to rest so you can be strong and recover."

I walked up to the hospital bed and held Vlada's hand.

"She was so beautiful," the friend said. "When she walked down the street all the men looked at her."

Helen, the aide, looked up from her magazine. "She always dressed nice, elegant."

"No, it's not that," snapped the friend. "She was beautiful. Look at her; she's still beautiful."

It was hard to see Helen's beauty. A nurse's aide came in and asked us to leave. The three of us walked out into the hallway. Vlada's friend said she had to go home. I also walked away.

Later that week in class, Alon spoke about Vlada. He said that he had been with her earlier in the week when she could still speak. Vlada was worried about who would say *kaddish* for her son, the prayer for the dead that is said on the anniversary of a person's death. She didn't have anybody to ask to say it. Alon told Vlada that he would say *kaddish* for her son—and for her one day.

Then Vlada spoke about all of the beautiful art in her home. "She doesn't have anybody to pass anything on to," Alon said. "But the only possession she really cares about is a gold necklace her son always wore. Vlada is leaving the necklace to Helen, the aide who has helped her for the past few years," Alon said. "I saw the way that Vlada held Helen's hand. Vlada said that Helen has been like a friend to her."

The woman with the white hair kept saying how alone Vlada was. But Helen was right by her side, and I hadn't paid attention. I had been looking in the wrong direction. So many of us are offered help and we don't see it. Maybe there was comfort waiting for me too all this time, but I couldn't recognize it.

Chapter 9

Drinking Coffee with a Patient

On Shabbat Seth and I invited our neighbors Valerie and Shimon and their kids over for lunch. I could hardly speak, like a sullen teenager who responds with one-word answers. It was as if I couldn't leave Vlada and the hospital behind.

I got up and went to the kitchen and returned with Moroccan spicy fish made with turmeric and cumin and peppers. Seth told a story about when he was a kid in third grade. He grew up in a small town in Eastern Connecticut. One day in 1960, his teacher, Mrs. Mary T. Shigrew, found him and four of his friends playing jacks on the bathroom floor. They were allowed to go to the bathroom but only one by one—not as a group.

The five of them sat on the bathroom floor in the midst of a jacks tournament. Mrs. Shigrew was very angry. She told them, "The reason that the Russians have Sputnik is because their fifth-grade boys don't play jacks in the bathroom."

Later he and his friends were given the job of taking care of the pollywogs in Mrs. Shigrew's classroom. The pollywogs lived in an aquarium filled with swamp water, and the fifth-grade boys were supposed to change the water in the aquarium daily by bringing in water from the swamp where they had gotten the pollywogs. But they forgot to. Mrs. Shigrew told them, "The reason the Russians have Sputnik is because their fifth-grade boys remember to bring the pollywog water to school."

We had to explain to all of our kids about Sputnik, the Russian satellite that was launched in 1957. But that story always made me laugh, the sheer absurdity of blaming fifth-grade boys for the Soviet Union's predominance in the Space Race.

It was such a relief to laugh. Later I went into the kitchen and brought out the dessert, a chocolate cake, and cut it for the sixteen people at our table. I felt grateful to have a full table, to have people to give to, to be surrounded by love and laughter. Still the hospital ward was on my mind, even here on Shabbat. But I was also able to appreciate my life which was full and rich—and right then, very delicious.

Michael told me that Musa was in isolation in Room 7112. He didn't mention that Musa was an Arab, but I knew that Musa was an Arab name. I'm sure that Michael had forgotten our conversation from the beginning of the year when he had asked me if I could work with Arab patients, because he offered me no special preparation before the meeting.

I walked toward the room and when I got to the door, I had to heave it open. It was surprisingly heavy. The doors were open to the other patient rooms, but the door to the isolation room was always closed. At first, I thought the heavy door was to protect those who wandered in the halls from getting sick. But I was wrong.

It was there, of course, to protect the patient from unwanted visitors and the infections that they could inflict. A row of thick white plastic ribbons like a shower curtain hung down the whole length of the door that I now stepped through.

I was not eager to enter. Of course, I knew that there were many Arabs in this and other Jerusalem hospitals. It's an irony of life here—we mix together most intimately when we are ill and dying or giving birth.

I gave birth to Koby in a Jerusalem hospital with an Arab woman in the next bed. Her extended family, the *hamula,* visited for many hours, bringing her large quantities of homemade food: pita, chicken, steaming pots of couscous and vegetables. They were so busy with their new baby and their delicious meal that they hardly noticed me.

I was afraid that Musa would stir up my memories of the horror of Koby's death. I didn't know what I would say. I thought that I might not be able to speak. But when I walked in, Musa was receiving a treatment; a nurse was in the room and she asked me to leave. Good, I thought. I'm off the hook. I don't have to come back.

But Musa said: *Please come back.* I told him that I was going to the kiosk to buy a coffee and he asked me to buy him a Turkish coffee—no sugar. I walked away and again wondered how I was going to talk to this man.

When I returned, I hoped that the nurse would still be there, and I could leave. But she was gone. I took a chair and handed him his paper cup of coffee. He was tall and thin and almost bald, his body seemed like it was all sharp angles, but his eyes were soft and large with flecks of gold in them.

He sat in a chair next to the bed and smiled at me, and the lines around his cheeks looked like a row of parentheses. He spoke gently, sipping his coffee. I sipped mine. I realized that I was drinking coffee with a patient. For the first time. Before this, the thought of drinking or eating in a hospital room had made me feel sick to my stomach.

When he spoke, his dark eyebrows lifted like birds. He told me that he and his family owned a cafe in East Jerusalem. He was in the hospital to receive a transfusion. He held what looked like a five-gallon size zip-lock bag of blood on his lap, the brilliant magenta of the blood a counterpoint to the pale beige of his hospital gown, the whiteness of the walls. For some reason, the blood didn't bother me. As he spoke, I noticed that he was hooked up to an electronic monitor that chirped and blurted red numbers.

A small rectangular blue and gray hooked prayer rug with the design of a date palm in front of a mosque was slung over the back of a chair next to him. I knew from the hospital sheet that Musa was 52, but he looked older. He told me that his wife had died of cancer a few years ago and left him with one child. He had remarried a younger woman and now they had another baby.

Even though his face was gentle, I was still afraid of speaking to him, afraid of all the history and pain that lay between us. He told me, "I was sick, and I got so tired I couldn't work anymore. I almost collapsed. They took me to the hospital, and I had a lot of tests, but it took a long time—almost a year until they discovered what the problem was—leukemia. I had a treatment last year, and now again the white cells are very low."

We sipped our coffees and he told me that he had had a bone marrow transplant last year, and now he was back, sick again. I asked, "Are you scared?" and he said, "No I'm not scared, God decided this and blessed is God."

I noticed that I was holding my hands together tightly, fingers clenched, and I let my hands fall open on my lap. I felt my fingers relax.

He added, "I'm happy even with leukemia. I'm happy because this is what God gave me and I love and accept what God gives me."

I felt my body tense. I rubbed my face below my ears in tiny circles because my jaws felt clenched at that moment. I didn't know how to respond. It didn't seem right to me to love God when he sent us so much suffering. I wanted Musa to protest, to cry out to God, to be angry. Perhaps this acceptance of death was a part of Islam. But then I thought—accepting what God gives you is also a Jewish belief.

I thought of Biblical Abraham and Isaac. God commanded Abraham to bring his son as an offering. Isaac was the son that Abraham and Sara had been waiting for, the miracle son that Sara gave birth to at the age of 90. Yet Abraham rose early, took fire and a knife, and he and his son walked to Mount Moriah where Abraham built an altar and bound his son. He held the knife in his hand to slaughter Isaac. Then God told him that he would spare Isaac.

It was a profound story of acceptance that I could not accept. Isaac was spared. My son wasn't. It's not surprising to me that a *midrash* tells us that Sara, Isaac's mother, died when she heard how close her son had come to death.

Of course, the story of Isaac was a foundational story in Islam as well as in Judaism. In Islam, though, from what I had learned, it was not Isaac who was taken to be sacrificed but Abraham's son Ishmael (from another wife, Hagar). In any case, both stories had to do with submission, acceptance. In fact, in the version in the Koran, Ishmael went so willingly he did not need to be bound.

I thought of the popular religious song: *It is a great mitzvah to be happy, to be happy always.* I could not be happy. I fact, I rejected the notion of easy happiness, but I knew that this acceptance of suffering and insistence on happiness was also a Jewish religious belief. I couldn't blame it on Islam.

I drank coffee while Musa's bag of burgundy blood lay on his lap. I didn't say a word about Koby, although I wondered what he would say if I told him. Maybe later; maybe another day. I wanted to ask him how men could trap children in a cave and stone them to death.

But Musa was smiling at me.

I thought of Yehuda, the man with Crohn's disease who had told me that he wasn't diagnosed with Crohn's—he *was* Crohn's. It had consumed him until it had become his only identity. Musa, on the other hand, was not defined by his cancer. He was not bitter. Musa was smiling, happily drinking coffee while holding his bag of blood on his lap.

Musa might not have been happy to hear that my sons would soon be soldiers. We probably had different political ideas. But speaking with him about his illness felt natural, extending a hand to somebody in need. It didn't seem momentous. I looked at the heavy door that marked Musa's room of isolation and realized that I could see that door as a message.

I had come to the hospital to make connections with people, but all of this time, I had been isolating myself emotionally in order to protect myself. I always felt that I was more wounded than anybody else. But something shifted that day. A door inside of me began to open.

Chapter 10

Naked

It was Adar, the month of joy, when Jews celebrate the holiday of Purim by wearing masks and drinking until we don't know the difference between Mordechai, the man of goodness, and Haman, the man who schemed the murder of all of the Jewish people. We leave our reason behind. On Purim children wear costumes, and we prepare food gifts for neighbors. We share a festive meal and drink. I had once loved the holiday of Purim. Now I found it unbearable.

In the beginning of the month, a group of 18- and 19-year-old girls from a local religious seminary walked around the hospital with their arms linked, singing—*He who brings in Adar enlarges happiness.* They brought spirit and cheer to the ward, but their presence seemed incongruous: it was hard to see happiness on this ward.

That day, I walked into room 7357. Michal, 62, lay in bed, her shirt off, the blankets covering her only to the waist. She was exposed, her breasts lay like small plump white pillows, untouched by the illness. She was completely bald with an oxygen mask over her face, and she was thrashing her body from one side of the bed to the other, holding on to the guard rails of the bed.

Then she stopped and lay on her back, looking at the ceiling. Two women stood on either side of the bed, as if they were standing guard. I was stunned by the scene: her nakedness, her distress.

"She's hot, and she can't get comfortable," said a woman with curly blonde hair down to the center of her back. She was wearing black linen trousers, a silk tangerine blouse and a huge jade circle pendant on a black cord. "She keeps tearing at her pajamas. So finally I just took them off her."

"Are you relatives?" I asked. The tubes of fluorescent lights above hummed and sputtered.

"I'm Michal's sister," the woman wearing the necklace said. "Revital."

"I'm Alona," said the other woman.

"Alona is Michal's best friend."

Alona wore tight jeans. Her red hair was parted on the side, an asymmetrical cut so that one side of her hair was much longer that the other. Her face was long and thin, a row of deep lines on her forehead looked like a grocery bar code. She looked pretty but her mouth had a hardness to it. Her lips were pursed in a straight line and her pink lipstick seemed too bright, especially in a hospital room.

"I volunteer here, doing spiritual support," I said.

"Michal, somebody's here to help you." Her sister looked at me. "Can you talk to her? Can you do something for her?"

I reached out for Michal's hand. But she wrenched it away. She was strong.

"Tell me about your sister," I said. Instead of offering a prayer or talking about God as I imagined other pastoral counselors did, I had decided that what I wanted to do in my work was to hear the person's story, give people the chance to tell me what the person was like before illness. Every person was a world, and knowing those worlds seemed important to me.

In class we had learned that Anton Boisen, the founder of modern pastoral counseling, called people "human documents"—a little cold perhaps. But I was starting to believe that a pastoral counselor's job was to open and share those "documents."

The sister immediately began speaking. "We're ten kids, a very close family. Michal is the oldest. It took her a long time to get married. She had a hard time having kids, so she adopted Dahlia.

"But when Dahlia went to the army, she had a psychotic break and she's been in and out of hospitals since then. And then a year ago, Michal's husband died—he drowned in the sea—and then she got cancer. She hasn't had it easy."

Michal lay in the bed with one eye open, one closed, her hands flailing. She thrashed her whole body from side to side and then suddenly opened her eyes and glared at us as if she had just realized where she was, or as if she were awakening from a nightmare, and then she settled back on the pillow and closed her eyes, her arms straight at her sides, fists clenched.

An orange tray with covered metal dishes sat on a chair in the corner of the room. Michal's sister stood and pumped on a lever with her foot to raise the head of the bed so that Michal could be more comfortable.

"Is it hard to see your sister suffer?"

"Yes, it's very hard."

"What kind of question is that?" said the friend. She crossed her arms and shook her head at me, back and forth so that one side of her hair swung.

I cringed from her disapproval, but she was right. That was a stupid question. I hadn't meant it as a question though. It was a statement in the guise of a question. I wanted to provide an opening, a gate.

Michal's eyes were still closed, her breathing more regular as if she was sleeping. Gently they covered her with the faded hospital blanket.

"Can you tell me about your sister, about a memory you have." The heater hummed, a machine gurgled from the other side of the room. A monitor somewhere kept beeping.

"A memory. She was such a wonderful sister," said Revital as she lifted the crumpled blanket and spread it out over her sister again. "She was so smart. She used to go to the movies and when she came home, we would gather around her and she would tell us the whole movie—from start to finish. We couldn't all afford to go to the movies.

"For Purim, she used to sew us costumes: Queen Esther, Vashti. And she's a scientist as well. A brilliant woman."

"It wasn't like it is now," Alona said, "where people buy costumes for Purim. Now people just go to a shop. But once everybody made their own costumes, wonderful costumes. I remember how my mother sewed me a queen costume. I did the same for my kids. It was a lot of work."

"She's only in her sixties, too young to be so sick," said Revital.

I sensed the idea of costume might resonate for these women. I said: "You know this time of year makes me think: Maybe the body is like a costume for the soul. Maybe we think we're our bodies when all the time the body is really a covering."

I realized that I was hardly breathing. I was afraid that I'd said something else stupid. But Michal's friend surprised me: "Yes, it's like that. It's really like that," she agreed. "You can't see inside somebody. You can't look at Michal now and see how wonderful she is. What a great friend she is, how giving, how generous. How smart. She was a professor of chemistry.

"And me, my husband died suddenly around the same time

that her husband died, and everybody looks at me and says—you look so wonderful, but they can't see inside, how hurt I am, how much I miss him, how lonely I am, how hard it is to go to family gatherings without him, to take care of the children. People don't invite me for Shabbat. They think that I'm okay. But nobody knows what's inside of me. How lonely I am."

"Sometimes you can't see another person's pain," I said.

"You can't see anything," Revital said. "We are so blind in this world. You just have to hope that God knows what he's doing. You just have to have faith." She looked at me and ran her fingers through her curls.

I felt like a mask had been removed. I told Michal's friend: "You lost your husband and now you're losing your friend."

"It's not easy," she said. "It hurts so much." Michal lay there quietly. I felt a raw and beautiful nakedness between Michal's sister and friend and me. I'd said something stupid; but even so, I had connected with them, allowing for deep feelings of love and sadness to emerge. I felt that intimacy, and I hoped that it was a comfort for them. It was for me.

Chapter 11

Imagining Death

A guest lecturer taught our seminar that week. Aviva, a family therapist, introduced herself. She was about my age, hair pulled back into a ponytail. Her voice was calm and soothing. There was something about her presence that gave me confidence in her, an authority in the way that she spoke, an inner balance that I wished I too could possess.

She asked all of us to write a dictionary definition of death. I wrote: *somebody whose life force has expired*. I thought of Koby. His life force hasn't expired. In fact, when people called the Koby Mandell Foundation office they sometimes asked for him: "Is Koby there? Or even, "Are the Kobys there?" So in a way, he was not dead, according to my definition.

Then Aviva asked us to write down expressions that described death. I wrote:

Dead as a doornail
Passed away
Passed on
Gone to his reward
Met his maker
Kicked the bucket

The others added:

Collected to his father (from the Bible)

Collected to his fate

We lost him

Became spirit

Aviva asked us to pick the expression that most resonated with us.

When it was my turn, I said, "I can't really say. All of these expressions seem better than the way my son died. In fact, the word *die* sounds pretty good. We don't usually say that Koby died. We always say he was murdered. There are no words here for that."

Alon said, "But he's dead."

"He was murdered," I said. "He didn't just die. He was 13 years old."

"Still he's dead."

Aviva jumped in, "I understand what you're saying—that these words describe a more tranquil death, a natural death."

I had brought up Koby's death in class just once in the beginning of the year when I told my story. But somehow with Aviva, I felt safe to speak about it. I realized that it was her presence, something in the way she listened that gave me the willingness to speak.

All of a sudden it was clear to me: sometimes it's not speech that creates listening but listening that creates speech. The way somebody listens, their silent presence, the feeling they give you of safety, can determine how fully we can speak and express our inner selves.

I trusted her. And I felt that I could do that for others on the cancer ward. I could be present in the same way that she was for me.

After Koby's murder, at the *shiva*, some people said: *I could never feel what you are feeling* while others said, *I know what you are feeling*. I didn't judge them if I felt the love and compassion behind their words. The words were filled with a person's presence, his or her lack of fear.

If they were afraid, I felt their discomfort and terror and that created a distance, no matter what they said. It was as if I had a sixth sense of reading their inner emotional worlds. I could feel who was safe. It had nothing to do with words.

All this time here in the hospital, I had been trying to find the right words, when really trusting people had to do with their presence, their lack of fear, their ability to come close.

Aviva continued: "Pick how you would like to die, or how you would want somebody else to die—one of the patients that you are working with. Write about it."

I thought that I would like to die in my sleep. But then I remembered that Seth's father had died in his sleep when Seth was 28, years before we met. Even though it sounded like a wonderful, painless way to die, you don't get the option to make amends, the chance to fix your relationships, tell people that you love them—there's no opportunity for healing.

In medicine there's a phenomenon called the hand on the door—the patient often doesn't reveal the most striking or telling symptom until he is almost out the door. So too, when a person knows that he may be dying, he can (often, with the right support) heal relationships, create intimacy, bring others closer to him in love. I know it's rare, but I had seen it with Rena's kids, who had told her that they loved her.

One family I met in the hospital told me that the father, who was dying of cancer, had been home for Shabbat and given special blessings to each person in his family at the Shabbat table. Each blessing, the mother told me, seemed a kind of prophesy of how the father believed the children should live their lives. He had blessed her to remarry and find happiness again.

I wrote:

I can't find a resting place, a place where my body feels okay. I am sore, aching, tired of this hospital, tired of my body. I want to leave my body, leave this world, to be free. I am waiting to be free, to shed this skin and disintegrate, return, die, be destroyed, become spirit, anything to be free of this pain.

The sores, the dry mouth, the pain, free me of the pain, passed on to another world, I will miss all of you, but I have passed on.

Jacob, a fellow student, who was sitting directly across from me, read what he had written about his own death—

"I wasn't born. Therefore, I don't die. I don't want anybody to be unhappy. If they are unhappy they can leave. I don't want anybody crying near me when I die. I won't allow it. I simply won't allow it. It's against everything I believe."

I couldn't help commenting: "But that's not fair," I said. "You're acting like a dictator. How about your children? You aren't letting them feel."

"I am on this earth to learn a lesson," said Jacob, leaning back in his chair, looping his arms behind his head so they folded out like angel wings. "Death is a teacher."

"Well not everybody is on that level. And it's not fair to expect other people to look at your death as the completion of a lesson," I said, rubbing my eyes with my hands.

"Death isn't good or bad, it just is," he said.

Jacob looked at me, brushed his hand out on the desk as if he was reaching toward me.

Ruth, a fellow student, told Jacob: "You know once you spoke about your father's death, and you cried. And it was beautiful to see you like that. You were vulnerable and you were somehow most authentic that way, most yourself."

Aviva knocked her fist against the desk and said: "Let's do a role play here. Who wants to be the daughter?" I surprised myself by raising my hand. "Sherri, you play the daughter and Jacob, you are the father who is dying."

"Now you can speak to him," she told me.

I was glad to do this because I felt that I had a lot to express. "Abba, I'm so sad that you're dying. It's sad for me. I want to cry. I have to cry."

"I know it's sad," Jacob said, "but please don't cry in front of me. You can meditate. I don't want anybody sad in my room. Death is okay." He rubbed his hands on his shaved head.

"But Abba, that's not fair, I'm sad. I'm sad."

"Don't be sad. The sadness bothers me."

"But I am sad. I can't change that."

Aviva interrupted us. "Tell him why you are sad."

"I'm sad that I won't see you."

"Why else are you sad?" asked Aviva.

"I'm sad that you're not sad. I want you to be sad that you're leaving me."

He started to cry. "I am sad, but I will be with you. I'll be with you when you sleep and when you wake up and when you eat and when you look at the stars, I'll be there with you. You won't see me, but I'll be there with you."

Ruth said, "How can you promise her that? How can you promise that you will be with her when you are dead? How do you know? You can't promise her that."

Jacob said, "Yes I can." He smiled as if she were a child who didn't know better. "Sickness and health are the same. They're both given to us to learn from. There's no difference between death and life."

"Come on," I said. "That's not true. Death is sad," I said. "Death is not passing on. Death is disappearance."

Aviva said: "Jacob, are you listening to your daughter?"

Another student, Varda said: "I want to say something. I don't want people to cry at my death, I want tranquility, completeness, not tears, I want happiness at my death bed, singing." She ran her hands through her curls, smiled at me.

"I don't know what the problem is with sadness," I said. "Why are people so afraid to allow sadness into the death room? Sadness isn't the opposite of happiness. Sadness can make room for happiness."

"I want people to sing when I die," Varda said. "I want them to sing me a beautiful song and for there to be peace."

"Death is just an opening," said Jacob. "A door."

And that was the end of the role play. Seth picked me up from work later and I was glad because I too exhausted to drive. I told him what had happened and how I felt that nobody understood me. Why were people so afraid of feeling? In telling me that only happiness was legitimate, they were negating my need for sadness at my son's murder, at all of the sadness here in the hospital. The role play hadn't helped me. Instead, now, I felt even sadder.

Chapter 12

Pastoral Care

Michael started the next study day with history. In order to understand the field of pastoral counseling education, we needed to know its creation story.

In 1920, Anton Boisen, a 44-year-old pastor, suffered from an unhappy love affair. While applying for a job that required him to write a statement of his religious experience for a possible ministry position, he became anxious, terrified that the world was headed for catastrophe, that gas and oil and timber would be exhausted and that he too was depleted, "a zero quantity," as he wrote. He was sure that the world was coming to an end.

He soon became manic and paranoid and his family committed him to a mental hospital in Boston, where he spent three weeks in a delirium. The doctors there diagnosed him as an incurable schizophrenic—paranoid, delusional, hallucinating. They told his family that there was no hope of recovery for him.

One night he looked out the screened window and saw the moon centered in a cross of light. For Boisen, the cross symbolized suffering—he saw the moon as a sign of the catastrophe and doom that he imagined was coming to the world. He was terrified.

But later he looked at the moon through another part of the

window —where there was a hole in the screen—and the cross disappeared. He realized that what he saw depended solely on the way he cocked his head, on his angle of vision. He could choose how to interpret the world around him. That insight marked the beginning of an almost immediate recovery.

He next asked his doctors if he could work in the mental hospital before his release. He became a photographer and was able to observe his fellow patients and the routines of the hospital that he felt were detrimental in many ways to the mental health of the patients. The pastors who visited the hospital gave sermons on Sundays but did not visit the patients on the wards. He began to believe that mental illness was the result of a religious crisis of faith and meaning, not just a physical or medical issue.

After his release, he felt a need to return to the mental hospital to comfort others. Since the field of chaplaincy education did not exist, he enrolled in a graduate program in theology at Harvard University and the Andover Theological Seminary.

From 1923 to 1924 he worked at the Boston Psychopathic Hospital, a hospital for the insane. The following year he entered Worcester State Hospital as a full-time chaplain. In 1925 he initiated the first clinical pastoral counseling training program, which gave pastors an opportunity to interact with patients as well as to attend staff meetings.

This program provided pastors firsthand knowledge of madness, and gave the insane the possibility of being helped by being heard and understood. His goal was to provide theological students with the opportunity to read "human documents" as well as books.

I was in the second cohort of pastoral counseling students in Israel. A few years ago, there had been no official field of pastoral counseling. Rabbis were in hospitals to decide questions of Jewish law like how to keep the Sabbath in the hospital, but not necessarily to tend to the sick.

There wasn't even a real name for us yet in Hebrew, because the word chaplain had Christian origins. We would most likely be called pastoral counselors or spiritual guides. But patients still didn't know who we were, or why we were visiting them.

The more we studied, the more I understood that pastoral counseling was a field without a coherent body of knowledge. The main thing we studied was ourselves. The hope was that in the course of analyzing the transcripts, we would grow more aware of ourselves: our inner conversations, what hurt us, angered us, and pleased us, our places of tension and friction. In this way, we would be able to help others without imposing our own issues.

That week Michael recommended the book *The Wounded Healer* by Henri Nouwen, a Dutch priest and theologian. I had already bought the book since it was on our reading list; that night, I read it eagerly. Nouwen claimed that we are all broken and that a minister (he doesn't use the term pastoral counselor, but the concept is the same) was a person with the ability to acknowledge his or her own wounds, places of pain and brokenness and loneliness.

He wrote that the Messiah, the redeemer who one day would bring peace to the world, was not described as a fighter, but rather as a vulnerable person. In the archetypal Jewish story of healing, the Messiah is a wounded beggar waiting with the other beggars at the gates of the city. I understood immediately that all of us trying to bring others healing—my teachers, fellow students, and me—we were all wounded healers.

Furthermore, Nouwen continued, we could think of healing as a form of hospitality, that a healer had to be able to concentrate on the patient, to put his or her own preoccupations in the background, to "be at home in his own house" and then healing could occur because we had carved out a space for the other person.

Being able to concentrate on the needs of another person was similar to the divine act of *tzim tzum*—when God contracted his infinite self in order to make room for the world, for humanity. Without *tzim tzum*, there would have been no space that wasn't overwhelmed by God's light. We too could contract ourselves to make room for the needs of another.

Reading this book comforted me. I was not alone, but following Nouwen's path. I, too, was a wounded healer who was learning to put my wounds in the background in order to concentrate on the needs of the patient. It was a relief to me when I understood that it was precisely my brokenness that would allow me to help others. I was a person who could comfort others not *despite* my wounds, but *because* of them.

Chapter 13

Strawberries

The first time I met Batsheva was in the middle of winter. The hospital was overheated that day: the air didn't move. The smell of old overcooked food hovered in the air. The trees were bare outside, except for the pines that held on to their needles. What a luxury, to hold on to what you are, not to have to change with the seasons, not to have to fall naked.

Stasis seemed like a delight to me, with all of the deterioration I had witnessed in the hospital. On the other hand, I realized that stasis could be a form of stagnation—not moving, not growing, not giving.

On the way to the hospital, I heard on the radio that Ariel Sharon was still in a coma. The government had changed, moved on. Ehud Olmert was now the acting prime minister. Sharon had lost his ministry, his majesty, his power. He was a patient in a hospital, like the rest of the patients here.

I bought myself a coffee to fortify myself and to put off the visits on the oncology ward. I heard the whirr of milk being frothed, smelled the heady shot of coffee as an antidote to the stale hospital air. The middle-aged woman who tended the kiosk was always busy and usually scowled. I put some change in the jar on the counter that said *tips*, and she smiled at me.

I realized that besides being a source of income, the tip was also a form of encouragement. Maybe the true job of a pastoral counselor was simply to encourage others. The root of the word *courage* comes from the Latin word *cor*, meaning *heart*. Every moment of encouragement could be viewed as waking the heart, rousing ourselves to believe and to have hope.

I waited for the elevator and then decided to walk up the seven flights of stairs. I put away my coat in Ora and Michael's office and saw a young woman sitting on an orange chair in the waiting area. She wore a red wool ski cap on top of her blonde shining hair and looked as if she could be headed for the slopes (unlikely in Jerusalem). She had large brown eyes with dark eyelashes so long they seemed fake, but weren't. She didn't look sick.

There was a free chair next to her. I sat down and said, "I'm a volunteer here. I do pastoral counseling. Do you feel like talking?"

"No, that's okay, I don't really want to talk."

I started to turn away.

"What does a pastoral counselor do?" she asked.

I thought for a second. "Here they take care of your body. Everything is so high tech, all the tests and the scans; well, we're low tech. I'm here to talk about what you are going through—what your mind and your soul are going through." She looked at me and smiled, small neat white teeth. "Can I sit down?" I asked again.

She patted the chair next to her. "What's your name?" I asked.

"Batsheva," she said. Through the frosted glass partition down the hall, I could see the room where patients gathered, reclining on chairs, receiving their chemo.

Batsheva told me that she was waiting to speak to her doctor, here for another round of treatment—after a few years of being free of cancer. I heard a trace of an accent. She told me that she and her family had made *aliyah* from France when she was nine. Then she began to tell me her story:

"The first time I discovered a lump on my breast I was 39 and pregnant. I got married later than all of my friends. I wasn't sure I'd be able to get pregnant, but I did. And then I had to have treatments and there was danger to the baby.

"At first, the doctors told me that I might have to abort because they thought the baby had kidney problems. They encouraged me to have an abortion. I didn't know what to do. But I decided to continue on with the pregnancy anyway. I prayed to God. I was operated on for the cancer two months before I gave birth. And the baby was healthy."

"You must have been so worried about the baby."

Her thick brown eyebrows arched as she spoke. "I tried not to worry. But I was so stressed. It was hard but thank God the cancer went away. My son is my life. I mean, I work as a bookkeeper. But my family is all that matters to me. Everything was going so well. It's been six years. And now I'm back here again.

"I was in a car accident, a minor one, and my back hurt. My mother was driving. I thought it was nothing, but the pain wouldn't go away. Finally, after a few months, I got it checked. They did some tests. The back pain wasn't from the accident. It was from a recurrence of cancer. That's when I found out. Thank God for the accident."

"It's unbelievable that something good could come out of an accident."

"You're right. It wasn't a big accident at all. But it might have saved my life."

We sat and talked about her son. He was in first grade. "It's hard," she said. "Sometimes I get so tired. But he keeps me going. I want to be there for him, like a regular mom."

"Does he know?"

"No," she said. "I don't want to upset him. I want him to have a normal mommy. I want him to have a normal life."

In my experience, children often sense when their parents are hiding something. They are smarter and more aware than we give them credit for. And besides, they absorb the cues non-verbally as well. So much of our communication occurs without our knowledge.

Batsheva said, "One day my son came home from nursery school and asked "Mommy, cancer is a bad disease, right? So I answered him: "Yes, but it depends on what kind and how it's treated and how brave the people are."

"You didn't want to tell him."

"No, I don't want to scare him." Batsheva was called into the doctor's office.

I worried about Batsheva's message of bravery. Bravery can't always change a disease from a bad one into a good one. Courage can help, yes. But I wondered if her son could be told that his mother was sick, maybe even that she was struggling to get well. He was probably already aware of that. Bravery is not always a comfort.

A few weeks later, I saw Batsheva walking toward the doctor's office, wheeling around the chemo pole with a flaccid plastic bag of poison that had exhausted itself. She sat down next to an Arab woman who was wearing a long brown gown, her head covered with a white *hijab*. The Arab woman had hazel eyes with spots of brown in them. Her skin was clear with a few freckles. Hands folded on her lap, she wore an amethyst ring on her pointer finger.

I turned and smiled at the Arab woman. I sat between the two women. "How are you today?" I asked the Arab woman. She said that she was fine. Then I turned to Batsheva.

"I'm so tired," she said. "So tired. I have no energy, I go back to sleep once my son leaves for school. And then when I get up, I start cleaning for Passover."

Passover is a holiday when many Jewish people rid their homes of all leavened foods—of all bread and crumbs—to commemorate the baking of matzah in the desert, when the Israelites fled Egypt and in their haste had to bake their bread quickly.

"But Passover is months away," I said. An older woman, a patient, walked out of a doctor's office, leaning on a young man, probably a grandchild.

"I have to get started because it will take me so long, because I'm so tired. I have to have everything clean. So I get up and do a little work. Yesterday I started cleaning my rugs."

"How do you clean them?" I asked. I was curious. Most people in this part of the world don't seem to have vacuum cleaners. The floors of houses are covered in tile, not carpeting. Sometimes on Friday afternoons, I could hear the loud, thwacking sound of people beating their rugs against the railings of their terraces.

She looked at me like I was a nitwit. "I clean them on the terrace. I take soap and water and I wash the rugs."

"But how do you get the soap out?" I asked.

"With a hose," she said.

It seemed obvious, but not to me as an American. We had carpeting all over our houses. We used vacuum cleaners.

The Arab woman suddenly perked up. "I just got a new vacuum cleaner," she said. "A special one. I haven't been feeling well and it's hard for me to clean too. When I invite guests, the house has got to be clean and I have to serve them."

I turned to her. She was also hooked up to an IV. "Having guests is good in a way," I said, "because it gets you out of yourself, but it's hard because you're tired."

"Yes, very tired. You can use this vacuum on everything—to clean rugs, draperies, the walls, everything." She searched for the bill for the vacuum in her bag, and showed us how much it cost. I told them about the new robot vacuum I'd heard about, one that worked all by itself.

The two of them said they both loved to clean when they were well. Both of their homes were spotless, but not now. Now, sometimes they had to rest all day.

I thought of the chemo that was entering their bodies, poisoning them at the same time that it cleaned them of cancer cells. Cleaning was a metaphor here. But I didn't think that they were talking about their cancer in covert terms. Talking about cleaning was a sign of normal life.

We sat companionably while the chemo dripped into their arms. Being women brought this sense of camaraderie in the face of disease and death. Beyond politics, beyond disease, there was the daily drama of a woman's life, working, taking care of the home and family, trying to fit everything in. I remembered my first patient, Liz, who only wanted to return to a normal routine; sometimes the ordinary became precious.

A month later I saw Batsheva again. She was sitting and reading, waiting for the doctor, her head down. She didn't want to speak. Then suddenly she turned to me, "It spread to my brain and my bones. The cancer. They found more growths on the scan. I'm forgetting things, I'm tired and I'm foggy."

"It's so hard," I said, feeling as if my own blood was plunging toward the ground. I felt suddenly weak. I was sad for her—and especially for her son and husband. "They want me to do an experimental treatment at Hadassah Hospital to shrink the tumors. I'll do whatever I can to beat this," she said. "Even though it's not a pleasant treatment. I'll have to be hospitalized for three days.

They do something nasty to your brain and the arteries from your heart. It causes a lot of pain."

After a few weeks when I didn't see her at the hospital, I called her at home. She said: "I got the results from Hadassah. The tumor didn't shrink. There's nothing more that they can do. The treatment didn't work."

Batsheva told me she was afraid, but she didn't give in to the fear. She tried to protect her parents from her harsh prognosis. She protected her son; she was in constant pain, but she kept her pain in the background as much as she could.

Her life—taking her son to his afternoon activities, picking him up from school—was still in the foreground. She didn't want to be in a cancer support group because she was so involved with her family and her friends. She had no time for a group.

Batsheva was referred to another doctor in Tel Aviv who might have another experimental treatment to offer her, so there was hope. Hope keeps our hearts from breaking. Hope is what animates us when nothing else can.

But it kept getting harder and harder for Batsheva to find hope. She was not eligible for that treatment. She didn't have the "right" kind of cancer. She was hospitalized for a fever. I visited her in the hospital. She had an infection in her lungs, and the port in her chest where she received her chemo was infected, red and raw.

Her parents were at her bedside, her mother with her grey-black hair in a low bun, her father next to her bed, both of them in their 70s, small, slow-moving. A basket of bright strawberries sat on the table that hooked over her bed. "Here take one," Batsheva said. "Eat." The strawberries were so lush, shining like they were from another kingdom, one where there was desire and appetite and beauty. They seemed incongruous in this dull room with its hospital bed and IV pole. The air in the room smelled bleached, antiseptic.

When Batsheva's father left the room, she told me, "He went all over town looking for medicine for my mouth sores. But I don't want him to give to me. I want to give to him. Eat some of these strawberries, please."

It was as if the strawberries had acquired symbolic significance—the fruit provided Batsheva with an opportunity to give to other people, to be a person who could offer others beauty, who could still act in the world, not just a sick person in a hospital bed. I ate a few. They were sweet and cold, but the sweetness didn't soothe me.

"Why don't you have some?" I asked her. But Batsheva shook her head no. She asked me how I was, what was going on with my family, what was new with my kids.

A week later, she was back in the hospital because she had fallen and injured her leg. She lay in bed and told me that she was in despair. She had been alone in the hospital for Shabbat. She was suffering, in pain. She said, "It's not okay to despair."

"Batsheva, you are always protecting other people," I answered. "But it's okay to be in despair. That's what you feel. Hope and despair, God gave us both feelings. You are carrying so much, trying to be strong for your parents and child."

"You're right," she said, and I could see her eyes fill with tears. It felt as if we had entered a holy space for just that moment.

A month later, Batsheva died in the hospital.

That afternoon, after Michael told me the news, I went home and got into bed without making dinner for my family and I thought, I cannot possibly carry on another moment in this hospital. I cannot deal with a world that is so cruel and harsh. Batsheva was lovely—and loving, offering everybody sweetness in the face of death.

Chapter 14

The Beauty that is Swallowed in the Darkness

It was a spring day, fresh, breezy, when I walked into room 7005. A large heavyset man who wore black pants and a green polo shirt sat on a chair with his legs sprawled apart.

His wife lay in the bed with her eyes closed, the head of the bed propped up. The chart said she was 64. She had large bow shaped lips and her cheeks were high, sculpted. A white scarf was tied loosely on her head. She tossed from side to side, turning her head. And then she opened her eyes. I told them both that I was a pastoral counselor.

He looked at me and asked "What? What do you do?"

"Spiritual support," I said.

"What's that," he asked in a gruff, angry voice. "What kind of profession is that? Did you study that?"

"Yes," I said.

"How long?" he asked contemptuously. He stood and took a handkerchief from his pocket and wiped his face.

"Since the beginning of the year."

"And what do you think you can you do for her?" he asked, turning toward his wife who clenched her eyes as she grimaced from the pain.

I didn't answer. I felt defensive. She was so horribly in pain. She was suffering, two deep vertical frown lines engraved in the space between and above her eyes. Then she looked straight ahead in a kind of trance. He rose from his chair and gave her a drink of water that she could barely sip from the straw.

He sat down again. "What can you do for her?" he repeated. "She already believes in God."

I was embarrassed. I wished there was something I could do to alleviate her pain. "I'm not a magician," I said.

"Well, what can you do?" he demanded. He stared straight at me, his mouth a thin line, his eyes streaked with red lines. "What could you possibly do to help?"

I paused before answering. "Can I sit down?"

"Yes," he said.

I took a chair. I sat. "I can be here, make a connection." I said.

"We have plenty of connections—we have a large family, children, grandchildren."

Well, I thought to myself. Good for you.

"I'll just sit here," I said, even though I felt his distrust and animosity.

I looked at her and the force of her pain overtook me like a wave that threatened to drag me out to sea. For a minute I felt dizzy, as if the earth was spinning too quickly.

That week in class we had studied this passage from the Talmud: Rebbe Elazar is weak and Rebbe Yochanan comes to visit him. Rebbe Yochanan sees that he is lying in a house of darkness. He uncovers his arm (Rebbe Elazar's) and light is revealed.

He asks: "Why are you crying?"… Rebbe Elazar says…"I am crying for the beauty that is swallowed in darkness." Reb Yochanan says to him, "For that you can surely cry," and the two of them cried together. The Talmud continues in the passage: *The inmate cannot free himself from prison.*

The woman looked at me with pleading in her eyes. "I'm wasting away," she said. I have no more strength." Her words entered me with the full force of suffering. I took them in, and I reached out my hand, and she reached out to me. I held her hand. That was what I could do. That was all I could do.

I sat and held her hand in silence. She squeezed my hand so tight it hurt around my wedding ring. I sat like this with her for at least fifteen minutes, looking at her as she stared into my eyes, looking at me, looking past me.

At the beginning of the year I had been so afraid of suffering. And here was suffering, and I was not running away. I was not trying to speak. I was not wondering what to say. I felt her pain and I knew how deep it was, and it scared me and I stayed with it. I felt the anguish of her pain. I looked into her eyes and I held out my hand.

The inmate cannot free himself from prison. I thought of all of the families and friends I had encountered on this ward: Reuven and his recipe, Batsheva and her strawberries, the siblings at their mother's bedside, Vlada's aide—the devotion I had witnessed. That devotion, that love, that beauty could not be swallowed by the darkness. That was what I had come here to witness.

Part II

Chapter 15

Moving His Lips

The following fall, when I was offered a job as a pastoral counselor one day a week at another hospital in Jerusalem, I said yes. The hospital was located a few blocks from a cemetery, as if death was the next stop from there. And it was, for a lucky few.

Most of the patients I worked with languished in the hospital, as if even death would not stop for them. They were patients in comas or in persistent vegetative states, which most doctors define as a person in a coma for more than a month.

There was no pastoral counselor to prep me at the hospital. After all, the field was new in Israel. Instead Anita, a social worker with no real knowledge of the field of pastoral counseling, supervised me the best she could—which was to inform me about the patients. Other than that, she couldn't really advise me what to do or say or give me much helpful feedback.

My first day of work, I went to Anita's tiny cubicle of an office to check in. She sat behind a desk with her back almost touching the wall. She handed me some forms that I was to fill out after visiting each patient. Then she sent me to visit Abe and his wife Esther. "She's a character," she told me. "You'll see for yourself. Let me know how it goes."

I walked down a long corridor, past a framed sign that said *all hospital personnel must wash their hands,* past a fire extinguisher propped against the corner of a wall in the hallway. I heard the familiar sound of buzzers and beeps. Room 241. I took a deep breath. I was anxious. I murmured my own prayer to God to help me.

I stepped in. The patient in the bed near the door was asleep. An older woman sat reading at the far bedside of the double room, near the window with its spacious view of the Jerusalem forest, dark groves of cedar and cypress and pine trees. Abe was 85, according to the hospital information sheet, and Esther looked as if she was also in her 80s.

As I stepped in to the room, Esther rose slowly from her chair and walked toward me. I told her that I was a pastoral counselor and asked her if I could visit. She said of course and kissed me twice on both cheeks, and then again. She smelled of baby powder and when she squeezed my hand, her own hands were warm and dry.

"Come sit with me," she said. The room had a vague smell of urine.

Her husband lay in bed with a pillow positioned under his chin, a pad of gauze placed there to catch the drool that slowly bubbled from his mouth. She repositioned the pillow. He, like almost all of the patients on this ward, had a breathing tube connected to his windpipe.

His arms were dotted with dull black and blue marks. I could hear the whooshing sound of the ventilator supplying him with breath. Bags of waste hung from the bed, and there were catheters and tubes snaking about him. His finger had what looked like a clothespin squeezed over it to measure the oxygen in his bloodstream. The ward outside his room had a muted cacophony of sounds—whispers, alarms, footsteps, bells, carts being wheeled by. But Abe was totally silent.

It was his eyes that most disturbed me. They had lost their color and were milky white and seemed to roll back in his head, so all I could see was a white glaze, no iris, no pupil. I felt sick to my stomach. What was I doing here? Part of me wanted to flee this room, this floor, this hospital, these vegetables.

Because that was what many people in the world called them. Vegetables. But I would learn that the word was not only crude, but inexact, erroneous. Language simply does not have the vocabulary to describe human beings in these states. As I looked at Abe, I wondered if he could think or feel, what kind of awareness he had.

I had read an article in the *New Yorker* that week about patients in persistent vegetative states. Scientists believed that these patients had more awareness than we credited them with. For example, researchers reported that patients in persistent vegetative states had sleep-dream cycles and parts of their brains seemed to be active.

Adrian Owen, a neuroscientist from England, asked a patient in a vegetative state to imagine herself playing tennis and then to imagine herself walking through the rooms of her home. With the use of functional magnetic resonance imaging, he found activity in some areas of her brain, the same parts that were activated in healthy volunteers who had been asked the same question.

Consequently, Owen believed that many of these patients did have some type of awareness. But nobody knew how much, and besides, the brain injuries were so varied that it was impossible to generalize.

I had also read an article in the news about a person who miraculously woke from his persistent vegetative state after ten years.

He told his family that he could hear them speaking all that time, but that he had no capacity to answer them.

When I looked at Abe, I decided to believe that there was communication on some level. After all, it was not possible to gauge the life force or consciousness of patients who couldn't communicate, couldn't move, couldn't express anything. When they couldn't eat or breathe on their own for years at a time.

I told myself that I would read hints and intimations: the blink of an eye, the pursing of lips. I wanted to believe that there was a relationship beyond words. I wanted to imagine that these patients had awareness. Esther, on the other hand, believed with all of her heart that she could communicate with her husband.

That day Esther told me, "I was saying prayers and Abe was saying them with me. I know because he was moving his lips."

I was skeptical. It was hard for me to see Abe moving anything at all. He lay as still as a dead butterfly pressed between the pages of a scrapbook. Esther said, "Abe used to love to pray. He got up at five every morning to pray." She took a sip from a glass of water and sighed.

"Yesterday the kids were here. And they were all upset because he doesn't respond to them. But he responds to me," she said. "I know that when I come in, he's happy to see me. I can feel it. His toes move. And his eyes move. I can tell because I know him so well. After all, we've been married for over 50 years."

I didn't know whether or not to believe her, but I wasn't going to challenge her.

Without any prompting, Esther began to talk about Abe. They were both Americans who had moved here to fight in the War of Independence. They met at an army base and after the war they got married in a simple ceremony. Her aunt had sewn her a wedding dress from the curtains in her home in Haifa. Abe later made his living as a teacher in Jerusalem, and they had three children.

She showed me the book she was reading, *The Palm Tree of Devorah*, a classic Kabbalistic text. "This helps me," she said. "I got this book in a really strange way. My brother has a very good friend named Murray who had a sister with cancer who was very, very ill—they only gave her a few months to live, and the sister went to a great rabbi who told her that she should read the book *Tomer Devorah* a little every day, and she would get better."

"The doctors gave her no hope. But she read the book—and now it's been over nine years, and she's fine. The doctors don't understand what happened to her. She was supposed to be dead in three months."

"So this friend Murray said he had the book in his house, and he wanted to give it to me to read to Abe. But he couldn't find it—and then he went to buy the book, but for some reason, no bookstore had it. He looked in every bookstore in Jerusalem. Even in Tel Aviv.

"And then—that same week, Murray and my brother were out in Tel Aviv late one night at a steak restaurant in Jaffa, and a beggar came into the restaurant, an older guy dressed like a Hassid with a black coat and hat, and they started talking and my brother gave him some money. The beggar walked away, but a few minutes later he came back into the restaurant with a book in his hand. He said to my brother, *"You know what to do with this book."*

It was the book *The Palm Tree of Devorah*. My brother came over that night with the book and gave it to me and I inscribed it to Abe—

To Abe, with hope that this book will bring you total healing. Love, God.

She looked at me. Her voice was soft as she asked: "Do you believe my story?"

"I do," I said. I didn't mention that I thought it was odd that she had inscribed the book as if God had autographed it. Instead I said, "Sometimes things happen that are just too coincidental. They can't be just chance."

I remembered all of the odd events that occurred after Koby's murder—many of them having to do with birds: birds falling dead at my feet, a bird in our car, a bird that flew into my head, dreams about birds.

I had learned in the Kabbalah that there was a bird's nest in the mystical supernal Garden of Eden, the most spiritual place in the world, where the Messiah waited to redeem the world; and in that bird's nest were pictures of children who died sanctifying God's name, children like Koby and Yosef.

"There's something in that book that you need to know, I guess. Do you want to learn it together?"

"Not now," she said. "But maybe another day."

Later that night at home, I read parts of *The Palm Tree* of *Devorah*, written in the 16th century by Rabbi Moshe Cordovero. The book is about how we can emulate God's attributes of mercy and forgiveness. It says that as God is merciful, we too should be merciful and that our doing good in the world gives God a kind of pleasure.

The title refers to the palm tree where the prophet Devorah sat as a judge, but it can also be read as an allusion to an oasis, a place of safety and sustenance in the desert. The idea of the oasis resonated for me. Perhaps that was what giving comfort demands: the ability to provide nourishment in the emptiness, to be comfortable with the wide-open spaces of conversation, to stand in the anxiety and desolation of another person's suffering, knowing that when it seems impossible to give nourishment, we can provide an oasis.

The next week when I visited, I showed Esther some cards I had with me that had excerpts from the Psalms printed on one side, and a photograph of trees or mountains or the sea on the other side. Each card was the size of a flash card, like the ones used for studying math or vocabulary. She read each of the Psalms out loud and then she turned the cards over to look at the photos.

"Beautiful," she said. She asked me for another card. I searched in my bag and gave her one more. Then she asked me for another one. She arranged the cards in one hand as if she was getting ready to deal a card game and plucked them one by one with her other hand, reading them out loud.

My soul thirsts for God. When oh when will I come and see the face of God?

You are the one who heals the broken hearted. You are the one who bandages their sorrows.

You open your hand and satisfy the desire of every living thing.

"Oh Sherri, I like these cards so much. Can I have them? Can I keep them?"

I said yes, even though I needed them for other patients.

"Can I have another to take home with me?"

I needed the cards. I was hoping to use them as springboards for conversation with the patients' families, but I said "okay," as if I was speaking to a child about candy or another TV show. "Just one more."

She read: *"And as for me, may my prayer to God be at a time of favor. Oh God in the abundance of your kindness, answer me truly with your salvation."*

"Can I have one more?"

I gave her one more and she stacked them together and found a rubber band in her white leather pocketbook to hold them together. "Can I please have one more?"

This was getting odd. I needed them. A man I knew had manufactured them himself and they were expensive. "I'm sorry Esther, but I need them for other patients and their families." She nodded and said that she understood.

Then she rose and kissed me, three times on each cheek, alternating cheeks. She walked over to her husband and stroked his face, saying: *Abe, Abe, my Abe. My wonderful husband. Isn't he handsome?*

Handsome was not the way I would have described him. I asked her: "When you look at him now, do you see him now, or do you see him as he was?"

"Both ways," she said.

"You see him in the past and in the present?"

She nodded. "Yes."

"Does it feel like maybe you are seeing his soul, as if the body is just a container? And you're connected to his soul?"

"Yes, that's exactly it." Her eyes filled with tears. "But I have reconciled myself to this, that if this is what God wants, then it's good."

"Do you always feel like that, I mean that it's good?" I pressed her.

"It's how I feel. I know that I can take this, surrender to it, with whatever happens. You see, I am in love with God, no matter what." She squeezed my hand.

"Of course, it's not easy. But this life, this life is so beautiful. There's so much to appreciate. Just the view from this window. The forest. There's so much beauty in the world. Even here, isn't there?" Then she got up from her chair and hugged me. When I said that I had to leave, she kissed me on one cheek and then the other, five times on each cheek. I didn't know what to think. But even in this awful room, she felt love, a love that transcended the body, a love that transcended the ravages of time.

On the way home. I had the beginning of a headache and a sinus infection. I stopped for miso soup and sushi at a Japanese restaurant on Aza Street, hoping that soup would make me feel better. I needed to rest before I returned home.

I sat there alone, trying to relax, sipping the warm miso broth with its pieces of tofu and seaweed. I watched two women chatting, eating, the conversation of ordinary friendship, a world away from the struggles of illness.

Then I thought of Esther. She was unusual, a character as Anita had warned me. But I realized that she reminded me of Musa: Esther, who insisted on seeing God's love in dire circumstances. She'd signed the book *Love, God*.

I knew that I was not like them. I was too angry at God to feel that unconditional love. I couldn't forgive. No wonder I had headaches and my stomach hurt. I couldn't believe in God's love when he had hurt us so.

Chapter 16

The Rock on the Well

The next week, I woke with a pounding headache. I felt pressure in my sinuses and my stomach was queasy. I was weak. I didn't have a fever, but I knew that I shouldn't go to work at the hospital where patients' immune systems were so severely compromised. I was disappointed because I wanted to see Esther.

I stayed home and boiled water and then poured it into a large mixing bowl with 10 drops of eucalyptus oil and stood at the kitchen counter with a towel over my head, my head poised over the large blue mixing bowl while I breathed in the steam for as long as I could stand it.

Then I lay on the cozy fake suede living room couch and looked at the blue frames around our three windows. When we built the house, the contractor showed me samples for the window frames and I had picked the color "pigeon slate" which, in the rectangular flip book of colors, seemed to be a bluish grey color.

But when the windows were installed and I saw their color, I was horrified. Bright shocking blue. I thought that I would never be able to live with them, that they mocked my staid and quiet character, the modest nature of our family. I soon learned to live with them. And now they are one of my favorite parts of the house.

I cooked chicken soup. I lay down and took a nap. I remembered my children's sick days, the opportunity for me to be home with them instead of at work. When I was a young mother, it was a relief sometimes not to have to go to teach at the university, to hang out and make tea and eat cinnamon toast with the children.

I remembered staying home myself as a child with my own mother, the flowered TV tray with the folding metal legs that she propped over me so that I could eat in bed, the long lovely afternoons when time seemed to stop and I could read or watch all the TV I wanted. And now I had a free day, home sick, and I wanted to go to the hospital to see Esther.

A day later, my stomach still hurt, and I woke with pressure in my sinuses. I went to my family doctor, who prescribed nose drops and antihistamines. And then a friend, a psychologist who was on bed rest during a difficult pregnancy, told me about a healer in Jerusalem and how much she had helped her. Even though I wasn't the type of person to go to a healer, my friend convinced me that this woman had vision and understanding and uncanny healing powers.

So the next Monday, I went to her office on the third floor of an office building in Givat Shaul. I told her my story. "I feel brittle," I said. "Like I could crack. I am carrying around this awful horror—my son's murder in front of my eyes."

She sat across from me in an armchair and said that she was going to check my energy field. She closed her eyes, making sweeping wave-like motions with one hand over the open palm of the other hand as if one hand were a plane that was performing aerial gymnastics. I wanted to laugh.

She told me that she could sense congestion in my body. She felt that there was a blockage in my lungs, a weakness in my spleen. I didn't trust her at first, but she gave me a cranial sacral treatment where she moved her outstretched hands over my body. She even put a plastic glove on her finger and massaged my gums and my mouth.

I began to relax. I began to breathe. She touched my body gently, and somehow it caused this enormous relief and release in me, a deep relaxation.

The next session a week later, she asked me to describe the pain that I felt in my body as a result of my son's murder, if I could put it in an image. I closed my eyes and saw an enormous rock, tons of rock, covering a well. My son was killed with rocks and there were rocks on this well, enormous rocks that would have to be moved by a gigantic crane in order for the well to begin to run again. The blockage was complete.

My well was stopped up. You didn't need to be a psychologist to understand that the well wasn't just a body of water. I was still blocked. Those rocks needed to be lifted and I didn't know how.

Then she asked me to imagine that image changing, the shape shifting, its edges blurring. Could the well change form? And if so, what color was the image that came to me?

I imagined a bouquet of balloons in a host of primary colors and then I saw an enormous hot air balloon drifting across the sky, I could see the fire burning under the basket propelling the balloon higher and higher, but I was in that basket, protected, and yet open to the sky. Soaring. I was buoyant, rising beyond the limitations of gravity. I flew gracefully, gratefully into the open blue sky. I imagined myself floating beyond the confines of this earth, floating above the world, floating toward God.

I walked into the hospital the following week and on my way to visit Esther, I saw a woman holding a bouquet of balloons, all different colors, their strings tied around her wrist. I looked at those balloons bobbing as the woman walked down the hall. In the midst of all of the suffering in the hospital, those balloons were a sign of play and freedom and joy.

I knew then that the healer had helped me. I felt ready to retrieve those feelings of joy I'd had before my son was murdered. I could imagine rising above the grief and the longing and the pain. Being happy. And I was sure that I had finally found the person I had been looking for. Esther might be one of the 36 righteous. Esther could be my guide.

Chapter 17

Singing to the Soul

In the mornings on the long-term care ward, some of the patients were brought out in wheelchairs to the outdoor plaza with its concrete patio and flower beds, a profusion of geraniums and wild roses. The patients lay propped in frozen postures, surrounded by the machines that kept them alive. They looked like artists in a performance piece where the artist doesn't move and isn't supposed to blink for hours at a time.

But here there was movement, although unsightly, involuntary: coughs, gagging, eye fluttering. The families and aides circled the patients, patting their mouths, wiping their noses, adjusting pillows and tubes, trying to make these patients comfortable.

In the afternoons the patients returned to their rooms, to their beds. Whenever I visited them, I would ask their permission to sit with them even though they couldn't answer me. I tried to respect their privacy and humanity. I sometimes read to them—children's books and essays by E.B. White.

Nobody from the staff told me much about these patients, but to me they looked as if they were poised in an in-between state, in limbo, neither in this world nor the world to come. They didn't look as if they were asleep. They stared and their eyes moved, and they sometimes grimaced or seemed to be in discomfort, but they were unable to move.

When I looked at them, they seemed to be relics of their former selves, like insects trapped in amber. They were trapped in limbo, seemingly dead while alive—yet they didn't have the luxury of residing in the underworld. For the first time I thought to myself: sometimes death is a privilege.

Occasionally I walked down the halls and felt like pulling all of the plugs from the sockets, disconnecting every piece of technology keeping these people alive longer than it seemed they should have been. In Belgium these people would have been euthanized. (In Belgium you can get euthanized because you are depressed. All you need are a few doctors to sign.)

One day I met Rebecca, a bereaved mother I knew from the Koby Mandell Foundation, on the patio. As I mentioned, my husband and I created a foundation in honor of Koby where we run programs for bereaved families. Our main project is Camp Koby for children, but we also run support groups for bereaved mothers and widows.

Rebecca was in our psychodrama group. Psychodrama, a technique created by Jacob Moreno, is also called theater of truth. This technique gives participants the ability not just to share their stories, but to witness them and also to change them. Our wonderful psychodrama teacher was always telling us to "trust the process."

Rebecca was tending to a young woman who had been in a traffic accident, the child of a friend. The young woman was in her early 20s and was now paralyzed and brain damaged, in a persistent vegetative state. Rebecca sat next to her, using cotton balls to wipe the young woman's face. She held her hand between hers, a tender gesture. She told me that there was little hope for the patient, but that her parents would not give up.

Later that afternoon, I walked into room 241, past the patient in the near bed who was curtained off, and approached Abe's bed. Esther stood up and waddled over to me and gave me a huge hug. She kissed me three times on each cheek. And when she was finished, she said *again*, and she kissed me three more times on each cheek. "For good luck," she said.

It was a bit confusing turning my cheeks the right direction. I thought all the kissing was getting really strange, but Esther was so enthusiastic that I was grateful for her affection. And there were many families on the ward who had no interest in speaking to me, so I appreciated her attention.

When we sat down, she offered me chocolate, but I said no. She was starting to insist when we heard coughing, choking, rasping and wheezing—she quickly rose and swept open the curtain that divided us from the other patient. She gave the man a cup of water from his night table, positioning the straw in his mouth. Then she put the cup back down and took a cotton ball from his bedside and dabbed at his lips. "Rami, it's okay," she said gently. "Bella will be here later. Don't you worry."

The man had black hair with grey at the temples. He looked much younger than many of the patients. Esther came back toward us and drew the curtain behind her. "His wife is never here. She's always working," she whispered to me. I could hear the judgment in her voice. Then she added: "But she usually comes later in the afternoon."

"I'd like to meet her," I said.

"Maybe she'll come today. Who knows?"

We stood next to Abe's bed: "Look at him, his toes are moving. He's happy to see us."

I didn't see anything.

"Sherri's here," she said to her husband.

We sat down. "I have such good news," she said. "My daughter-in-law had a baby." Then she turned to her husband: "Abie, Yael gave birth. A cute little boy. He looks a little like you. I'm going to a *brit* tomorrow. And there's also a bar mitzvah, Jacob's bar mitzvah."

She told me: "Our grandson. Look at Abe. Look at his eyes, his eyes moved. He hears me. He knows. He's happy too."

Again I didn't see anything. But I said, "You still have communication. You are still connected to him."

She opened her big black purse and took out a bar of chocolate and snapped a cube off. "Here Sherri," she said. "You have to eat some. We need to celebrate."

I put out my palm. I didn't want to eat in this room, but I had nowhere else to put it—it was already starting to melt—so I put the chocolate in my mouth. It was creamy and sweet.

"I'm so happy," she said. "A *brit* and a bar mitzvah in one week."

"That's wonderful," I said.

She stood up and took my hand: "I have someone special I want you to meet. Goodbye sweet Abe," she said. "We'll be back soon."

We walked down the hall holding hands, past the rows of patients in their rooms, past the little kitchen, and the soda machines, and the orderly sitting on a chair reading the newspaper, "I think you might be able to help her," Esther said.

We passed an empty wheelchair, passed the nursing station. Esther led me to a room at the end of the corridor. The door was closed. She turned the knob and we walked in. There was just one bed.

A young woman was lying there, her head bandaged with white gauze so that she looked like a mummy. She was propped up with towels on both sides of her head, staring straight up at the ceiling, her mouth open as if she were shouting. Sun streamed into the room, spotlighting her. The woman's face reminded me of the famous silent scream in Edvard Munch's painting. Esther stood next to me and whispered, "This is Kayla. Such a young woman, so sad, she had a stroke during childbirth with her second child. The baby died—and look at her..."

Anita, the social worker who supervised me, had told me about this 27-year-old patient. I had wanted to visit her, but Anita told me not to, that there was no help I could possibly give to a woman with such severe brain damage. And besides, the family didn't want anybody they didn't know visiting Kayla, especially when they were not there.

I looked at Kayla. I wondered if I should leave—of course I should leave; but when I looked at her, I felt that I had to stay to try to help her. She seemed to be in such discomfort, as if she were crying out. I walked closer to her.

Above her bed on one of the shelves was a photograph of a woman holding a child, a cute boy with round black eyes. In the picture Kayla was a beautiful young woman, laughing, her eyes were wide and bright, her blonde hair in braids. Today she was drooling; her face a flat round moon as she stared at the ceiling, one eye fluttering closed. Her breathing, even with a ventilator snaking from her neck, seemed labored; her face was white. She seemed to clench her eyes closed, as if she was in pain. Esther took a paper towel from the dispenser on the wall and gently wiped her mouth. We stood and looked at Kayla. What was there to do?

"Should we be here?" I asked.

"It's fine," said Esther. "I come here every day."

Then she whispered to me- "Maybe we could sing something. What do you want to sing?"

"I don't know," I said.

She began to sing *Hush Little Baby,* a lullaby from my childhood, and I sang along. We held hands. "Hush little baby don't you cry, mama's gonna sing you a lullaby…Hush little baby don't say a word…Mama's gonna buy you a mockingbird. And if that mockingbird don't sing, Mama's gonna buy you a diamond ring. And if that diamond ring turns brass, mama's gonna buy you a looking glass…"

I had sung this song to my kids at night. But I had never before sung to a patient. I remembered my teacher, Michael, asking me if I could sing to a patient. I didn't think I could sing in a place like this. But as I sang with Esther, her voice strengthened mine. We kept singing, laughing as we lost track of the verses.

Kayla's breathing slowed. It seemed as if she were listening but there was no way to know. Kayla closed her eyes and seemed to relax and rest. We kept singing and my voice felt strong for once. And then Kayla's eyes fluttered and opened, and she closed them, and she soon nodded off to sleep. Her body was quiet.

The next week when I arrived at work, Anita said that she wanted to speak with me. I walked into her teeny office and sat down. I was nervous, sure that she knew. And I was right. Immediately she told me that she had heard that I had been in Kayla's room with Esther and that the family said that it was forbidden and that I was not to visit again.

"What did you think you were doing, going against my orders? You knew you weren't supposed to visit!" she said, leaning toward me, her dark bangs covering her eyes.

"You're right." I said. It was so unlike me to disobey authority. I couldn't justify my visit.

"She can't hear what you're saying. She's almost dead. What were you thinking going in there to bother her?"

"I went with Esther," I said. "We sang to her."

"You should not listen to Esther. She can be very inappropriate.

She's not staff, Sherri. You have to be more responsible. Kayla can't hear you. She's totally unresponsive. You know that, don't you?"

I nodded. But I didn't agree.

"The doctors say that there's no brain activity. She's brain dead. The family deserves their privacy. I expected more from you. I'm shocked at you—that you would do such a thing. And don't do it again."

"I won't," I said.

I did feel guilty for disturbing Kayla—but only because it was against her family's wishes. On the other hand, I was glad that I had visited her because I felt sure that she had heard us, that we had comforted her. I was reminded of a statement I had read in Martin Buber's book *10 Rungs*, a collection of Hasidic sayings: *When a man is singing and cannot lift his voice, and another comes and sings with him, another who lifts his voice, the first will be able to lift his voice too. That is the secret of the bond between spirits.*

I had felt that bond both with Esther and with Kayla. Esther had helped me raise my voice to sing. Kayla couldn't speak, yet it felt that we had discovered a bond between our spirits, a moment of connection beyond the limits of this world.

Chapter 18

A Form of Madness

At this hospital I kept learning that there were things worse than death. One of the patients, a 38-year-old man named Baruch, had completed his doctorate in comparative religion and celebrated by taking a vacation in France with his fiancée. They were riding a motorcycle on a winding mountain road when they were hit by a truck, the motorcycle careening down a cliff.

She was killed and he had been in a vegetative state for 12 years, his brain bashed in, so even to look at him was painful, the bones of his skull dented in on the top right. Devorah, his mother, a second-grade teacher, visited him every day and every time I spoke with her, she cried.

There were others on the ward, like the woman with ALS who could communicate only by blinking; and another woman, a concert pianist with ALS, who didn't communicate at all—by choice.

So it was always a relief to find Esther to talk to. But that Tuesday she wasn't there. Her husband lay back on the bed, his eyes milky white, his mouth open, a towel rolled up next to his neck, propping his head in place.

A visitor sat on a chair on the other side of the double room. I assumed she was Rami's wife. Rami was out of bed. He sat in a wheelchair, next to her, his pajamas wrinkled, blue slippers on his feet.

His wife sipped coffee from a paper cup. The rich potent smell filled the room. I walked over to them and told them that I was a pastoral counselor. "Would you like a visit?"

Rami's wife nodded and I sat down. She told me that her name was Bella. She wore an orange shirt and a green skirt, bold colors. I took a chair and sat next to her and she told me that she worked as an interior designer. "It's hard for me to come visit during the daytime. But today I had the day off," she said, "so I'm here visiting my honey."

She looked at her husband. "Rami's recovering from a stroke. He's beginning to move and speak—not like these other poor people. He's only 50, so we're hoping for a full recovery. I'll be able to take him home soon, thank God."

She took a sip of her coffee and sighed. I could see steam rising from the cup. "This coffee is good."

She looked over at Abe. "Poor thing. Did you meet Esther?" she asked me.

"Yes."

"Her husband had a terrible stroke," she said. "He's never going to recover. Poor thing."

The wind suddenly whipped against the closed windows and then subsided. Bella poured some coffee in another paper cup, blew on it, and gently tipped a little into her husband's mouth. "Don't tell anybody," she said. "He's not supposed to have coffee." He swallowed softly and smiled. "I'm happy that Esther's not here," she continued. "Thank God. She drives me crazy."

I didn't say anything.

"You know, with the kisses."

"She does like to kiss," I said.

"I'm glad not to see her," she repeated, taking her husband's hand in hers and massaging it, opening a tube of cream and smoothing it gently all over his hands. The milky vanilla smell of the cream filled the room.

Again, I didn't respond. I didn't like criticizing Esther. I wasn't going to criticize a patient.

"All that kissing. It's not normal. And the chocolates. She's excessive." She put her husband's hand back in his lap and wiped her hand with a piece of paper towel that she snatched from the wall next to the sink.

I didn't like the turn the conversation had taken. Maybe Esther was excessive. But I thought she was wonderful.

"You know she has dementia."

"What?"

"Oh, yes, you can ask anybody. She suffers from dementia. And it's getting worse. She has to leave her apartment in Jerusalem so that she can move in with her daughter. She can't live alone anymore." She picked at the cuticle of her thumb.

"Dementia?"

"She's not all there," she said. "Haven't you noticed?"

"No," I said.

I felt like a fool. I knew that she was unusual. But I didn't think that she had dementia.

On the way home as I drove through Jerusalem traffic, I wondered if Esther really had dementia. If so, I'd been looking at somebody with a brain disorder as though she were my teacher. I was disappointed—I had imagined that she could be one of the 36 righteous who could lead me to happiness. What could I have been thinking?

And then I remembered: Boisen founded pastoral counseling because of his madness. I thought about how the prophets in the

Bible sometimes entered a trance that could seem like madness in order for them to hear God's voice. In Hebrew the words for praise (*hallel*) and madness (*hitholel*) are connected. If you're too sane, too stone cold sober, how could you ever praise this world? Maybe you had to be a little bit disturbed to love life and God with such abandon. Maybe you had to be a little bit mad to bear the suffering of this ward.

I knew that it was time for me to stop taking everything so seriously, to let go. It was time for me to laugh at the lack of logic in this world, the way that so little made sense. My suffering had made me bitter and brittle.

I had been working so hard at finding comfort—as if I were a miner who had to chip away at a massive rock to arrive at the nuggets of wisdom I was seeking. I was exhausted. Maybe instead of trying so hard, I would have to become a little mad. Maybe I could learn from Esther.

Chapter 19

Kissing Back

Isaac held on to the hope that his wife would recover, even though she had been in this hospital for almost nine years. Edna lay in bed with her eyes open, yet it was doubtful that she could see anything. She had once been a concert violinist.

Now after a heart attack that left her deprived of oxygen for too long, she was attached to a host of tubes including a ventilator and a feeding tube. She didn't respond to people's voices, to the nurses, to the doctors, or to her family. Isaac was retired from his job as a high school biology teacher, so he came to the hospital every day to be with her.

Isaac had already told me parts of their story: Edna's family had lived in Jerusalem for 11 generations. His own parents had fled from Germany before the war, but his father's parents and siblings had all been murdered in a concentration camp. Issac had fought in the Israeli army in three wars. His best friend had been killed in battle. Isaac said that he was lucky that he had survived.

I sat on a chair next to the hospital bed, as Isaac patted his wife's lips with a gauze pad. Then he took a washcloth from a drawer in the table next to the bed. He walked to the sink, wet it, squeezed it out and cleaned her face and hands. Next he took moisturizer from the night table and massaged his wife's feet. The warm smell of vanilla was a welcome reprieve from the antiseptic smell of the hospital room.

"The nurses here are wonderful," he said. "But I also like to take care of my wife. I can't leave her alone here. She would do the same thing for me."

I looked around the room. He had set it up as if it were an office: a table with a laptop and stacks of books, a computer chair, and a standing lamp.

He said, "You know my children don't want me to spend so much time here. They hardly come and visit. But I can't get angry at them. They're so busy with their lives. They want me to go back to work, to travel, to do something else. But this is my job. I can't leave her. I know she would do the same thing for me."

I agreed with his children. Maybe it was time for him to stop spending so much time here. I decided to broach the subject but before I could, he said, "Today though I have to leave early. I have a dentist appointment." He smoothed the blanket out over his wife and kissed her on the forehead. Then he bent down and kissed his wife on the lips. And I witnessed something unusual, so unexpected—shocking. His wife's lips seemed to close and purse and brush his.

"Is that what I think I saw?" I asked him as he wrapped a scarf around his neck, his body stooped.

"Oh yes," he said, looking at me. "Go figure. It's the only thing she can still do. And I don't think it's just a reflex. Maybe it is. But she seems to want to kiss me. I mean she puckers her mouth."

He bent down and put his lips to hers, and she kissed him again. A small pucker. Light. Gentle. Her lips pressed together. I couldn't believe it. She was a person who seemed almost dead, and here she was, kissing.

It wasn't the story of Sleeping Beauty. In fact, it was the opposite. Edna was not going to wake up. But there was a part of her, I knew it now, that had never gone to sleep. I remembered a verse from the Song of Songs: *I am asleep, but my heart is awake.*

I felt as if that statement included Edna and Abe and even my son Koby. A person could seem asleep, even dead, but there was always a part of them that was awake—the soul. A piece of eternity, a touch of God, something that could never be destroyed, was here in this room, hidden in this bedside kiss.

Chapter 20

Ordinary Death

A month later my mother died suddenly at the age of 79, most likely of a heart attack. She had not been in good health for the past year. I called my mom the day before she died, and she told me that she didn't feel well. Her stomach was bothering her, and she was weak. I told her to rest, that I would call her later that night to check in with her.

She stayed home with Verona, her aide. And then my mother felt that she couldn't walk, that she might collapse. Verona called the ambulance. On the way to the hospital my mother told one of the medics on the ambulance crew how cute he was. I know that if she was still flirting, she didn't suffer for too long.

She died 20 minutes later in the emergency room. When Verona called my sister after my mother's death, she cried because she loved my mother.

My 16-year-old daughter Eliana flew with me to New York for the funeral. In the crowded cemetery in Fort Lee, New Jersey, my sisters and I rode in a limousine toward the section where my grandparents and father and my mother's baby brother who died when he was a week old were buried. It was cold, though it was almost spring. I shivered in my coat. Buds sprouted on the trees overhead.

I saw my father's grave. My mother had picked these lines from a Liza Minelli song for the inscription on his headstone:

It was a good time
It was a great time
It was a party just to be with you

For my mother's gravestone, my sister suggested the next verse:

And we believed that it would last forever
We'd stay together and share the laughter

The inscriptions were so different from the one on my son's grave—in Hebrew, a passage from the Torah: *He (Jacob) dreamt and beheld a ladder, set up toward the earth, and the top of it reached to heaven, and behold, angels of God ascending and descending against him.*

My life had taken me very far from where I had begun.

After the funeral, we returned to my sister's one-bedroom apartment on 14th Street in Manhattan to sit *shiva*. So many people came to visit us there. And then at night after everybody had left, a phone rang, and it wasn't my sister's phone or my phone. It kept ringing.

I searched for it, and found it in my sister's jacket, my mother's cell phone. My sister had brought it back from Florida. It felt strange to answer my mother's cell phone. A voice said, "Hi."

"Yes?" I said.

"It's Rafael."

I recognized his voice, my mother's boyfriend.

"I'm in Florida," he said. "But I'm calling because I wanted to hear your mother's voice on the message."

When I got back to Israel, I stayed home in bed for two days because I wanted to give myself time to mourn. I missed my mother, calling her, speaking to her, the way she loved me like no other person. I thought about calling her cellphone, the way Rafael had done, but I didn't. I didn't need to hear her message. She had given me a gift. I would always have her voice inside of me—a voice of love.

I finally felt compassion, real and deep, for anyone who had lost a relative or friend, for anyone who was suffering. In my work at the hospital I had thought of myself as a wounded healer, but my wounds had overwhelmed me, and it had been very difficult for me to offer real empathy.

The loss of my mother, while painful, was normal and manageable. This loss would bring me closer to other people, to being able to comfort them. In this way, it was a comfort.

Chapter 21

Dual Citizenship

It was forbidden for me to enter. Anita had told me not to venture down to the children's ward downstairs in this hospital for very seriously ill children, most who were in persistent vegetative states—kept alive with breathing and feeding tubes. She said that the children's ward was the most difficult ward and I needed more experience before working there because it was devastating to see children who would never get well.

But then there was a terrible accident in my town. A child from my neighborhood, a beautiful one-year-old girl, Halleli, strangled in the cord of the curtains in the nursery school before her caretakers noticed. She suffered severe brain damage and was on life support. When I visited her family in Hadassah Hospital, her grandparents told me that she was being moved to the hospital where I worked.

That day in March I told Anita that I was going down to the children's ward, that there was somebody I knew there. She said, "I'm so sorry to hear that. Take care of yourself down there."

"What do you mean?" I asked.

"You'll see. It's heartbreaking there."

I walked down the stairs to the children's ward and opened a set of heavy double doors. I was afraid of what I would see but when I entered the reception area and looked into the large open ward, at first all I noticed were walls decorated with playful drawings of Walt Disney characters like Snow White and the Seven Dwarves.

I asked a nurse behind a high counter where Halleli was, and she told me that she was not being transferred here. Since I was already there, I poked my head into the ward: children attached to breathing tubes lay in cribs. I saw a beautiful young woman wearing a long blue skirt and a crisp white tailored shirt sitting next to a crib. Two children stood on either side of her.

I took a few steps in, past the sink with a box of plastic gloves next to it, past the hand sanitizer dispenser on the wall. I told the young woman that I was a spiritual support person. She said that she was with her kids and it wasn't a good time for her to speak with me.

But the next week, I ran into this same woman in the main lobby of the hospital and she said: "I'd like to talk to you." And that is how I found myself on the bottom floor, working with the children's families once a week.

There I met Michael, a three-year-old boy who had been beaten unconscious by his mother's boyfriend, an actor and psychopath who wanted the child to be silent. His mother and her boyfriend were both in jail now. This boy, Amir, could no longer breathe on his own. He lay in bed under the covers, with his sweet face untouched, his long black eyelashes fluttering.

I imagined him as a prince in a story, one who has been sent away from the palace and gotten lost, wandering in a dark forest, trying to find his way back home. I sat by his bedside and sang him songs like *the eensy teensy spider climbed up the water spout* and *I'm a little teapot*, so playful, so incongruent with the horror of his life. He was battered by the people who were supposed to protect him.

Chaim, a sweet red-headed boy, was attached to a breathing machine because he had had a stroke. I didn't know that a four-year-old boy could have a stroke. Another boy had stopped breathing at birth and been revived. He was brain damaged, his mouth was twisted, his skin a map of purple blotches, he drooled constantly. His limbs were stiff and rigid, fixed in what looked like an unnatural, impossible position. His mother had adopted him as a baby. She was a single mother who wanted to care for a child nobody else would care for, who needed her. There were people in this world who were simply extraordinary.

A few weeks later I met Amina. She was thin and wore leather sling-back heels, tailored pants and a silk shirt with a scarf tied over her head and around her neck. She had high cheekbones, large brown eyes, olive skin. Her lips curved down at the edges.

I learned that she was 23, from East Jerusalem, the mother of two children. She stood next to her son's crib. Yasir was critically ill. At birth he was deprived of oxygen and he was brain damaged. He was also blind and deaf, periodically sent to another hospital in Jerusalem for emergency care.

I visited Amina each week even though we didn't have a common language. She spoke Arabic and just a few words of English and Hebrew. We hugged a lot. I felt the bones in her shoulders.

One day she said to me: "Why don't you learn Arabic?" I laughed to myself. It was a good idea, but I had to improve my Hebrew first. I hadn't known many Arab women. And I certainly hadn't hugged very many. Hugging became our language.

We stood by her son's crib. She lowered the metal railing to take him out. She held him and combed his hair. She wiped his face clean with a baby wipe. He was chubby with apple cheeks and large lips shaped in a cupid mouth, a beautiful looking boy. She was always busy tending to him: changing his diaper, putting clean overalls on him. The oxygen meter flashed its busy important numbers and we stood there together, at her son's side.

Each time I visited, we hugged. Sometimes she cried. We had a relationship that was not based on words but only on caring, on being two mothers. I saw how she suffered watching her son. "Not good," she would say, "not good."

One day when I walked in, her husband was there, on the other side of the bed. It was the first time I'd seen him. He was tall with dark hair, no beard, wearing a t-shirt and jeans. Each of them was on one side of the crib, holding Yasir's hands, stroking his face.

I looked at the two of them and I knew, by the intensity of the feeling in the room, that this was a deathwatch. I walked in and she turned to me and hugged me: "Should I stay?" I asked her. "Yes, yes" she said. I hugged her and she cried, her thin body trembling.

A nurse carrying a clipboard strode in and tried to shoo me away. She wore a white uniform and her white tie up shoes were newly polished. "What are you doing standing there?" she asked. I told her I was a pastoral counselor. "You can't be here," she said.

She was a nurse I had never worked with before. She didn't even know that there was a profession of pastoral counseling, that there were pastoral counselors working in this hospital. I left the room and talked to the social worker who spoke to the nurse. When I returned to Yasir's room, that same nurse said to the family: "She is here to do a spiritual intervention."

I shook my head. No. I was not there to do an intervention. I stood with Amina. I wasn't trying to enforce some kind of pastoral care agenda. I held her and she cried onto my shoulder and she kept crying. I felt the sadness and the despair and the longing and the love.

    I, who had lost my child to Arabs, stood with Amina and hugged her in her loss and cried with her. We were two women, two mothers, beyond words, beyond politics, beyond nationality. I felt her tears on my chest.

Chapter 22

Becoming a Patient

And then, just when I was learning to sing in the face of sadness, to find compassion, just when I needed to work in the hospital because I was finally finding healing, I had to leave.

I still didn't feel well. In the past, I'd stayed home from work or stopped at the sushi restaurant after work to rest before returning home because I had a headache. I'd gone to the healer, but I still had headaches and stomach aches and sinus aches.

I visited a doctor in Jerusalem, a physician who trained at Harvard and also studied Chinese medicine in China. He treated me with acupuncture for my sinus infection. He thought that the sinus infection was connected to my upset stomach and recommended that I be checked by a gastroenterologist and have a colonoscopy.

A month later I prepared for the colonoscopy. My husband drove me the 25 minutes to the clinic, the hospital that was once a maternity hospital, the hospital where Koby was born. I remembered the night I gave birth, wandering in the garden there because they wanted to send me home. I'd rushed to the hospital after an hour of labor, sure I was ready to give birth. Instead it turned out I was dehydrated and that's why I was in so much pain.

Now I waited in the clinic and when the nurse finally called me in for the colonoscopy, I pushed open the double doors and I was surprised because there was a row of hospital beds there, some of them with curtains drawn around them. The nurse asked me to change out of my clothes. Suddenly I was a patient, vulnerable, exposed in my flimsy gown.

I lay in bed and the nurse brought me a permission form to sign on a clipboard. I read all of the possible side effects and dangers and deliberated before I signed the permission form. There were so many possible complications—perforations and bleeding and the risk of death, that I was tempted to leave the place and forget about the procedure. In fact, I called my husband who had already left the hospital and told him I didn't want to do it.

He advised me to go ahead. I'd already been taking laxatives for two days, cleaning my system out. I wasn't about to do that again. I signed the form and about twenty minutes later an orderly wheeled my bed down a hallway, turning a sharp corner into a room lit by bright lights for the procedure. The doctor asked me to turn on my side and administered a shot that put me out.

I woke when the doctor pulled back the curtains and stood next to my bed in the clinic with a clipboard in his hand. Seth was there as well. The doctor wore a white coat and in his lovely South African accent he said: "I have some news for you." With his soothing accent and the afterglow of the tranquilizer, I didn't think it would be bad news. "I found a polyp that is not the good kind. It's a …villous adenoma." I had no idea what he was saying. But I heard the rest: "I couldn't cut it out. It's flat against the skin. It could be cancer. So you will need to schedule a procedure to have it taken care of in the hospital."

"What?" I looked over at my husband who reached out to hold my hand.

"You are the person that we do all this screening for. That's why we recommend a colonoscopy for everybody. If we don't take out that polyp, it could lead to cancer. But we can probably prevent you from getting colon cancer. You're a lucky woman. You can be cured."

After I went to the surgeon the next week, I didn't feel so lucky. He sat across the desk from me and with a pen and the back of an envelope sketched a diagram of the colon and the stomach and said that I would have to be in the hospital a week and they would remove a portion of my colon.

"There are many meters of colon," the surgeon said. He was originally from Chile and his accent might have charmed me if I hadn't been so anxious. "You don't need it all. Don't worry. You'll be fine."

I was terrified. I realized then how much courage all the patients I visited had because I had none. I was so afraid that the cancer would be malignant and that I would have to wear a colostomy bag. That my stomach would bloat up like Liz's, the first woman I had visited in the hospital, that I would never be able to eat again and that I too would die just when I was beginning to live.

A week later, Seth and I met with another doctor, a private specialist in Herzliya, and he too told me how lucky I was. Still, I broke down crying in his office. He recommended another colonoscopy at Tel Ha Shomer Hospital, telling me that there was a chance he could remove the polyp at the same time, so that I wouldn't need an operation.

The next week, I took the laxatives, ate the special diet, and Seth and I rose early and drove the hour and a half to the hospital, hoping this doctor could remove the polyp during the colonoscopy. Instead when I woke from the anesthesia, he told Seth and me that there were six polyps, that I would need the operation in Jerusalem.

I felt hysterical, I was so anxious. All this time I had thought I was an expert in suffering and I now understood that I had only been a bystander in the hospital, a person who really didn't get it. I hadn't learned anything from the courage of the patients I'd been working with.

The surgery was scheduled for a Sunday morning. I was supposed to arrive at the hospital on Saturday night. That Saturday I ate a meager diet and felt the anxiety weighing on me. On the way to the hospital, we stopped at the Western Wall, the Kotel, and I sobbed to God for fifteen minutes, begging him to make sure that I would be okay, that I would be able to stay alive for my family.

We arrived at Hadassah Hospital at about 10:00 pm and I had to drink eight liters of water with a laxative in it. Seth went home and my 20-year-old daughter Eliana stayed with me until he returned in the morning.

I didn't have a room but was parked on a bed in the hallway, up all night running to the bathroom with its sandpaper toilet paper. The orderly who helped me was named Jihad, which I did not find reassuring.

In the morning, after a nurse gave me a pill with ten milligrams of Valium, they wheeled me into the elevator and then into a stark bright operating room that was so cold I couldn't stop shaking. The staff were wearing shower caps, their shoes covered in plastic booties. The lamps looked like five enormous jelly fish. The farthest wall was painted with purple flowers. I felt as if I'd been taken to a strange and distant planet.

They'd taken out many inches of my colon. My daughter Eliana spent the first few nights with me, sleeping on a hard, wooden chair next to me. When I woke up the first morning, she held my hand. "You were squeezing that morphine drip all night. How do you feel now?"

"Better." I didn't have much pain.

A few hours later, they took the morphine away. Eliana sat next to me, reading, speaking gently to me. I rested. I had never been so grateful for anybody's loving concern. I believe I had less pain because she was with me.

A sock-like plastic apparatus on each of my legs periodically squeezed and released my shins to prevent blood clots. A huge line of staples ran down my belly. I couldn't eat anything for five days. I was hooked up to an IV.

And then I realized how clueless I had been, like in the Sufi story where a man can't tell how delicious the food is for dinner until he himself has tasted it. In the same way that others couldn't understand the profound experience of losing a child, I didn't really comprehend what the patients I'd worked with in the hospital and their families endured.

It was not until I was hospitalized that I realized how awful it was to be here: how painful, how fraught with stress, and anxiety and horror. How a person who was turned into a patient had so little control. How so many of the patients I had visited were exemplars of courage and love.

And something else surprised me: I didn't want visitors. I needed quiet in order to heal. I gave permission only to family and closest friends to visit. When a friend visited and spoke on her cell phone, I felt violated. I understood what an intrusion a guest could be when you were hospitalized. Only then did I grasp the gift that the patients in the hospital had given me: sharing their presence, even when they were so vulnerable.

I had been welcomed into their sanctum. It was a much larger gift than I had realized.

Two days after the operation, I was sitting up in bed, the hospital gown wrapped around me. A group of doctors on their morning rounds came to examine me. They looked at me and the doctors talked to each other, but they didn't say anything to me. Nothing. They did not offer me any comfort. I could have been a sickness instead of a person. I said, "Please tell me who you are," and they told me their names. Then they walked away. I suppose, luckily, I wasn't that interesting a case.

Later an aide came to my bed, dressed in her green uniform, pants and a tunic. She had a full head of black curly hair and she was smiling, her lips were cherry red. "Come, Mommy," she said to me. Mommy is a term of endearment in Hebrew. By her accent I could tell her native language was Arabic.

"Where?" I asked.

"I'm Fatima. I'm going to give you a shower."

"I can't take a shower," I said. "I can hardly walk."

"I will help you," she said.

She removed the apparatus from my shins, releasing each strip of Velcro. "One leg and then the other," she said.

I leaned on her and put one leg out of the bed and shuffled into my slippers. I held the hospital gown closed and shuffled into the bathroom, and she waited while I undressed. "I'm not going to leave you," she said. "I will stay here with you. Just call." Her words were a comfort. They also reminded me of something. The words seemed familiar.

She opened the shower curtain and adjusted the water.

With her help, I got into the shower. She tested the water before she handed me the nozzle. "Is that the right temperature?" she asked.

"Just perfect," I said.

"There you go, Mommy," she said and walked out. I showered and the water felt so wonderful. As I tipped my head up to let the water pour onto my face, I remembered what she had just said: "I'm not going to leave you. I will stay here with you." Those were the words of the ideal visitor I had imagined in class, the one I had written about.

I hear footsteps.
I want someone with an open face...
"I am not going to leave you," she says. "I will stay here with you. I will stay here by your side."

Fatima was not a doctor, not a nurse, not a pastoral counselor. Yet she was the one who knew what to say to me to help me feel better. When I was finished, I called her and she helped dry me from head to toe, toweling my hair firmly the same way I used to dry my babies.

"Now there, Mommy," she said. "Don't you feel better?"

I got back into my hospital gown and returned to bed. I did feel better. And I understood: you never know where your comfort will come from, but there are always those who will offer it to you, always those who are willing to help you. It could happen, anywhere, anytime.

I had thought that I needed to meet one of the 36 righteous in order to be initiated into the secrets of how to overcome suffering. Instead, comfort was made up of small moments of care and connection—small stitches of love. Comfort was available to all of us when we allowed ourselves to receive it.

I recuperated in a large room with four other women in varying degrees of abdominal disrepair. Across the room, the picture window offered a view of the valleys of Ein Kerem that were blossoming with the first almonds. In the far corner bed lay a young, thin Palestinian woman with large brown eyes. She lay there without moving very much but she cried a lot.

In the mornings, she looped a tan scarf over her head and neck and read from the Koran. Sometimes she prayed by heart. One afternoon her younger sister, a slight woman wearing jeans and a t-shirt, came to visit and slept in the bed with her all night. These young women spoke only Arabic. I couldn't talk with them.

After four days, the day before I was to be released, the Palestinian woman's husband, Mahmoud, visited. He was a young man, wearing jeans and a button-down blue shirt. I spoke with him in Hebrew. He told me that his wife, Aya, was the mother of four. A Palestinian doctor had botched an operation for a problem on her pancreas and now the Israelis were trying to save her. He had put the children in an orphanage in Ramallah.

"She lost all of her small intestine. She'll have to be on a feeding machine the rest of her life," he said. "She can't eat any solid food." Then he told me that he didn't want to marry again although, as a Moslem, he could take another wife. Instead he rented a new apartment in Ramallah on the ground floor and bought Aya her own fridge and washing machine so she could be comfortable when he brought her home.

Then he said, "I'm told that there is a transplant possibility in Germany or America."

I thought for a moment. Then I said, "I can look into it in America for you."

I asked for his number. I said I would be in touch, that I had a friend who was a gastroenterologist in New York. "I hope we can help your wife."

He translated for his wife. She smiled at me. When at the end of the week, I left the hospital, I gave her the presents my husband and my friends had brought me: teas and cherry lollypops, hand cream and my new box of tissues. "Thank you," she said awkwardly in English, her lips arching into a smile.

Five days after the operation, the day they released me, I was finally able to eat again, and they served me cream of wheat in a plastic bowl on a hospital tray. It tasted so delicious to me, totally plain. I felt grateful for life, for each moment.

When I was wheeled out of the hospital I felt as if I was seeing the world for the first time, the almond trees luscious with white bloom, the smell of the air with a tang of citrus, the wind brushing my cheeks like the softest caress. It was a miracle to be alive.

While I recovered at home that month, I spoke to my friend, the doctor in New York who told me that he needed Aya's medical records from the doctor in Israel. So the next month while I recuperated at home, I tried almost every day to reach Aya's surgeon from the hospital. He never returned my calls.

I called Mahmoud, Aya's husband. We conferred on her case. He told me that he worked in a bakery and would bring me bread. I told him that I would try to get his wife help. I wanted her to be able to eat again. To live again.

I kept calling but the surgeon in Jerusalem wouldn't answer my calls. Finally, at my post-op appointment, I talked to my own surgeon who was the head of the trauma department. He told me that Aya was not a candidate for a transplant. She could not be helped. I called Mahmoud and told him the disappointing news.

We didn't have a TV movie ending, an Arab and a Jewish family joined together in an act of kindness—a woman who had lost her son to Arab terror saving a Palestinian mother. No, we weren't featured on Oprah. Nobody wrote an article about us or paid any attention. I had not been able to save her. But I had tried.

During that same month, I reread the book *The Wounded Healer* and realized that I had misunderstood an important part of the text. I hadn't paid attention to the section where Nouwen writes that if we are able to touch our brokenness, we also come to know that being alive means being loved. And we comfort each other from that place of love.

I had witnessed that devotion again and again, as families cared for their loved ones in the hospital. That love transcended the fragility of the body. That love defied death. It was a holy eternal love like the love that we declare in the blessings before the Shema: *With an abundant love you have loved us HaShem our God, with exceedingly great compassion...* Each relationship in our lives held the capacity for a sacred encounter.

All this time I had thought that I was helping others from my brokenness, from my wounds, my knowledge of death. But now I understood that it was the love that I felt toward others that created compassion. It was love that gave me the ability to comfort others, to listen to them and feel with them, and support them—to stand with them on holy ground. Love was the source of comfort—not only my pain, as I had once believed.

During the month I recuperated at home, my friend Valerie accompanied me each day for a short walk. After a few days, I could make it down my block, past the two-story stone houses up to the entrance to the canyon with its view of the Judean Hills, the canyon where Koby and Yosef were murdered.

Each day we increased our walking time because I was preparing for the first Koby Mandell Foundation fundraising hike which would take place six weeks later. I had no idea if I would recuperate enough to participate. But I love hiking, and I wanted to do it.

The week before the hike I was able to walk a mile. The day of the hike, I boarded the bus going north with the other participants and told myself that I would do what I could. That first day we walked in beautiful country near the Banias nature reserve with its stunning waterfalls. We splashed through the shaded paths of the Snir River in our water shoes.

I was elated to be moving, in nature. I jumped in the stream in my clothes. The water was freezing cold and I didn't care. It was running fast and a bit wild and choppy and I floated on my back as it pulled me downstream. I hooted with happiness. I knew that world was like that water, wild and unpredictable—and I was again willing to relinquish myself to it.

There are many ways that a well can be blocked. It can be frozen, or it can be filled with stones, or it can be overgrown with plants and weeds. Sometimes the water in the well is running but we can't reach it; our bucket doesn't descend far enough into the vital waters. Then we may have to tie lengths of rope so that we can dangle the wooden bucket closer to the underground springs and retrieve the pure water.

I knew that each person I had visited in the hospital had been like a length of rope that had led me to being able to dip a little deeper, so that I could finally bring the wooden pail to the surface and drink the refreshing water, to feel alive, to let go of the weight of my son's dead body.

I was so happy to hike, to appreciate the trees and flowers: the jack-in-the-pulpit wildflower with its wave-like architecture, the hyacinth squill, and clusters of delicate red poppies. I felt that I had been sewn together, restored, given another chance to truly appreciate the splendor of ordinary life. I walked with my husband on the narrow path as we began to climb a grassy hill together.

I had finally emerged from the underworld. I felt a kind of ecstasy at being joined to nature, to life, to others. The word comfort is from the Latin—and means with strength—*con forte*. I had found my strength.

I knew the euphoria of my survival would not last, but I had learned this much: I no longer had to dwell in the land of suffering, in the underworld. I had gone to the dying to learn how to live. To find comfort. And all this time it was the world of the living—my husband and children and family and friends and the wild beautiful earth, nature, mountains, sky, trees, grass, flowers, streams, birds—that had just as much to teach me.

I didn't know if I would return to my work in the hospital. My doctor advised me not to. He said that the world was too hard on me. That I had enough to face with helping the bereaved mothers and children of the Koby Mandell Foundation. But I knew this much: If I was going to offer comfort to others, it would have to come not only from my understanding of suffering, but also from my love of the wild holy beauty of living.

About the Author

Sherri Mandell received a National Jewish Book Award in 2004 for her spiritual memoir, *The Blessing of a Broken Heart*, which was translated into three languages and adapted into a stage play. She is also the author of *The Road to Resilience: From Chaos to Celebration*; *Writers of the Holocaust*; and two children's picture books, *The Elephant in the Sukkah* and *The Upside- Down Boy and the Israeli Prime Minister*. A certified pastoral counselor, she is co-director of the Koby Mandell Foundation which runs healing programs and camps for bereaved children. The foundation was created in honor of her son, Koby, who was murdered by terrorists in 2001 when he was 13 years old. An international lecturer on grief and resilience, she lives in Israel with her family.

You can reach her at sherrimandell@gmail.com

CPSIA information can be obtained
at www.ICGtesting.com
Printed in the USA
BVHW032232220321
603236BV00009B/201